THE SUNDAY TIMES

IMPROVING EMPLOYEE PERFORMANCE

Nigel Harrison

KOGAN PAGE

This edition published in 2009

Kogan Page India Private Limited
4737/23 Ansari Road,
Daryaganj
New Delhi 110 002

This edition is for sale in the Indian subcontinent only. Not for export elsewhere.

ISBN-10: 81-7554-454-6
ISBN-13: 978-81-7554-454-3

Published by Vinod Vasishtha for Kogan Page India Private Limited,
4737/23, Ansari Road, Daryaganj, New Delhi 110 002.

Printed and bound by Raj Press, R-3, Inderpuri, New Delhi - 110 012.

contents

1

introduction

This book is about improving employee performance and closing performance gaps (the difference between what people are doing now and what you want them to do).

Most of us never really analyse the issues that we have with our staff, our colleagues and our teams. In this book we will diagnose the reasons for performance gaps and find solutions that will stick. Most of the problems that we are fixing today are yesterday's problems that come back to haunt us. It can be very satisfying to solve the fundamental problems rather than applying yet another quick fix.

When I was a new line manager I thought that problems with people were too complex to understand. I hope, like me, that you will be delighted to know that there is a simple process to understand employees' performance and find real solutions for real improvement.

This book is for managers. We will look at some practical theory, introduce a simple process, and work through some real examples.

My aim is to show you that this process works and that by using it you can tackle any performance gap.

two approaches

The chief executive had a problem with employee performance. She set it to her two best managers:

> 'Our middle managers are not creative enough. Can you do something to help them?'

Manager One commissioned an international expert on creativity to come in and run a creativity workshop for the managers at enormous cost. The managers enjoyed the sessions and said that they got a lot out of it. Six months later the chief executive challenged the manager:

> 'What value did we get from your training? Our sales are still down compared with the competition. The press says our products are stale and haven't changed for years! What good did that training do?'

Manager Two, in contrast, challenged the chief executive:

Manager Two: 'What would it look like if the managers were more creative?'
Chief Exec: 'Our product range would be fresher for a start.'
Manager Two: 'How would you measure this?'
Chief Exec: 'Our competitors have 40 per cent of their range as new products for this season. Our figure is 15 per cent.'
Manager Two: 'What would be the effect if we do nothing?'
Chief Exec: 'Our sales figures will continue to fall, these managers are under threat and so is my job!'

Manager Two explains his approach:

> 'Well, I didn't accept that the problem was the creativity of our managers. Instead I got them together and presented the problem. They

were amazed that there was a difference in their product refresh rate compared with their competitors. They thought the chief executive wanted to see continuity and had often given the subtle message that she did not want too much change.

'I facilitated a session when they came with their own action plan. Some of the managers read up on new product campaigns and creative problem solving and they shared tips and hints with each other about what worked.

'All in all their strategy worked. I think it was because we didn't assume that the chief executive had diagnosed the problem correctly. In fact all she had done was give us her version of the solution.'

This illustrates a common problem in organisations – the rush to find quick fixes and instant solutions. We call it 'solution-eering'. Manager Two solved the problem rather than implementing an instant solution. Which manager are you, and which one would you like to be?

Instant solutions are never successful on their own. The only way to guarantee success is to understand the causes of the real performance problems and implement integrated solutions. This book will show you how.

what will I be able to do?

When faced with a need to improve employee performance you will be able to follow a seven-step process to:

- find out who has the problem;
- define the cost of the performance gap; and
- design a set of solutions to close it.

the seven-step process

1. What is the problem?
2. Who is involved?
3. What is happening now?
4. What do we want to happen?
5. What is the cost of the gap?
6. What are the causes and potential solutions?
7. Action plan

is it hard work – do I really want to do it?

Try the questions below to see how much you want to read this book.

brief self-analysis

- *Why are you reading this book?* Be honest! This is for your needs only. No one else will see it.
- *Who is involved in this?* Put yourself in the middle of the box and draw a diagram to represent your clients, colleagues, boss and anyone else involved.

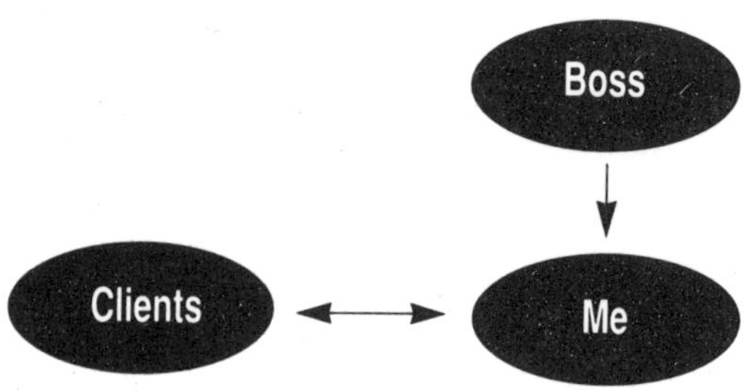

- *What happens at the moment?* How do you improve employee performance at the moment? (Are you Manager One or Manager Two?)

- *What would you like to happen?* In, say, 6–9 months' time? How would you like to be solving performance problems?
- *If you do nothing about this gap what will the cost be to you?*
- *What would be the value to you of closing the gap?*
- *Is it worth doing something about?* If the answer to this question is no, you will be better off reading something of value to you. If the answer is yes, carry on reading.

You have just completed a brief performance-gap analysis on yourself, asking who is involved, what you are doing now, what you want to be able to do, and what the cost of the gap is.

This is the first step in improving performance of any kind.

2

why do we get performance gaps?

what is a performance gap?

Virtually any sort of problem can be described as a performance gap – the difference between the current state and how we would like it to be – and it involves people in some way.

Actually I think all problems are fundamentally gaps in people's performance. Try to think of one that does not involve people:

- Nuclear accident – is about the operators and management safety culture.
- Car exhaust falls off – involves the owner of the car who did not have it serviced, driver, passenger and garage mechanic who has to fix it.
- Software glitch – affects the users and involves the help desk in trying to help and programmers to fix it.

Performance gaps can also be performance opportunities, eg a successful sales team who want to achieve even more next year.

what is performance analysis?

Have you ever listened to a manager telling you that a member of their staff needs training or a transfer? At the back of your mind you probably wondered if this was the correct solution. Doesn't it all seem a bit too easy? What is the real problem behind this need? That line manager is '**solutioneering**', that is, going straight to an assumed solution without analysing the real causes for the behaviour.

In Performance Analysis we analyse the causes for a performance gap before implementing solutions. It is sometimes called '**diagnostic problem solving**'.

The diagram below summarises two different approaches to problem solving: the diagnostic approach and the quick fix.

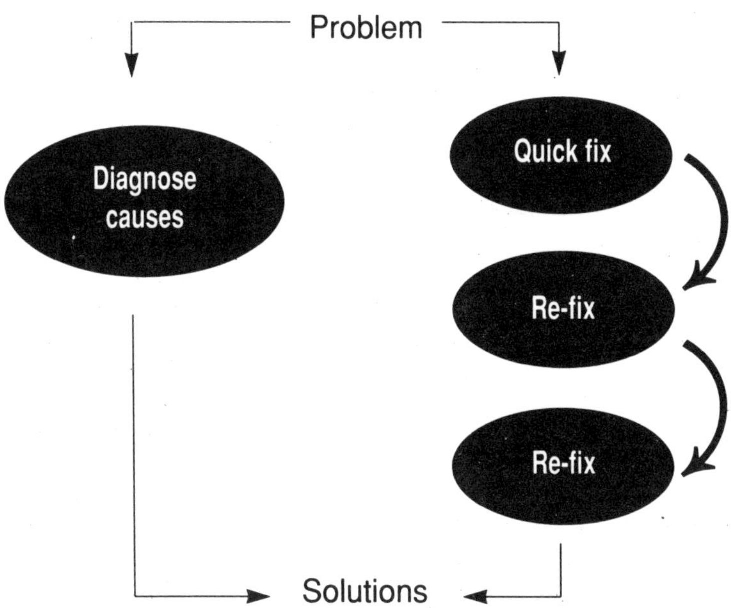

Both of these approaches have their strengths and weaknesses.

Diagnostic

Strengths	Solutions based on causes are most likely to work first time.
Weaknesses	Can take time, 'paralysis by analysis'.

Quick fix

Strengths	Allows instant action and the impression of progress.
Weaknesses	You can waste time fixing the wrong thing.

The ideal solution is a fast diagnostic phase followed by quick action. However, it is human to solutioneer and to avoid rather than face the real problem.

a real example

The sales director of a bank was worried about the sales of insurance products. In order to improve figures he asked all branch staff to double the number of leads that they passed to the insurance sellers.

At the end of six months the bank staff had achieved their targets (and received a bonus) but the sales of insurance products had actually gone down.

lessons

- The only analysis done was by the sales director who also designed the solution: 'We need more leads.'
- The middle managers acted as mere 'order takers' and did not analyse the real performance gap.
- Without any analysis of the original performance gap, the bank invested in a spurious solution.

This sort of 'non-analysis' goes on all the time but in most cases the results or lack of them are never reviewed; usually it is not in anyone's interests to do so.

This is a classic case of quick-fix problem solving. The only good thing about this process is that it is fast.

The key lessons in avoiding solutioneering are:

1. Find the real problem.
2. Diagnose the causes.
3. This will tell us the correct solutions to invest in.

a mythical case study: Old World

Let us imagine a fictional company called 'Old World'. In Old World, line managers receive support concerning their staff's development and training from the personnel and training department. This company reflects the old values of the workplace, when jobs, knowledge and skills were fairly static, unlike now, where roles are no longer fixed and skills needed are ever changing.

Imagine the personnel director (Peter) commissioning the new training from Fred, the training manager:

Peter: 'Fred, I'm glad I caught you. I've just come from a board meeting, and the executive is worried about our lack of project management skills. Can you organise some project management training for all our project managers as soon as possible?'

Fred: 'Well, all my trainers are very busy at the moment, but I know that Prosaic Trainers do a good project management course. I'll get on to them, but it could be expensive.'

Peter: 'Let me know how much to train all our project managers within the next six months.'

Fred: 'Okay, I'll get back to you by next Monday.'

next monday

Fred: 'Hi Peter, I've done a TNA on that project management training you wanted. We have 150 project managers throughout Europe. Prosaic can run a five-day course for up to ten delegates; they can run it in major cities but we will still have to fly some people in to central locations. We need $350,000 for Prosaic's fee to run 15 courses plus $200,000 for travel and accommodation. We will run one pilot course to test the content; do you want to attend? Is the budget okay?'

Peter: 'I'll put it to the board on Friday but I don't see a problem; they're pretty worried about our project management. Well done, Fred.'

Fred: 'No problem, Peter.'

two months later

Peter: 'Can we review how the project management training is going, Fred?'

Fred: 'Sure, we have everyone scheduled to attend a course by the end of the year. Fifty people have attended so far and the feedback is good. Prosaic certainly know their stuff. Some of our guys say it is a little too complicated for their use but most said they learnt a lot. The big groups are a bit of a problem but the trainers are all coping well. Great feedback on the food and the hotels, everyone seems to be enjoying the courses and getting a lot from them. Everyone says it's a good opportunity to get together with colleagues from other locations. It's all going fine.'

the end-of-year review of training expenditure

Peter: 'Did we hit our targets for that project management training and how much did we end up spending?'

Fred: 'Yes, we got everyone through, although it was a bit of a push; we had to schedule one extra course for people who had missed their slots but they're all trained now. The feedback sheets show 75 per cent satisfaction; some people thought it a bit too long but all rated the trainers as expert in their topic. The costs overran a bit, as the total bill was $600,000.'

one year later

Peter: 'Fred, I've had a tough session with the board – they say that our projects are still an average of six months behind schedule and 20 per cent over budget. Frankly, they are saying that the training we did was a waste of money. They want us to explain what value we got out of our $600,000 investment last year. In fact, they want us to justify all our expenditure on training this year and link it to bottom line improvements.

'As a start they want you to reduce your headcount by 50 per cent over the next three months. I am sorry about this, and, to make things worse they've gone over our heads to employ some high flying performance consultant to investigate the reasons for the project management delays and failing to meet the budget!'

Fred: 'But we delivered everything they asked for!'

the lessons from this case study

- The only analysis done was by the board, who also designed the solution: 'We need project management training.'
- The personnel director and training manager acted as mere 'order takers' and did not analyse the real performance problem.
- Without any analysis of the original performance or any criterion for what they wanted to achieve, it was impossible to evaluate the effectiveness of the training.

does this sound familiar?

This sort of non-analysis goes on all the time, but in most cases the results, or lack of them, are never reviewed; usually it is not in anyone's interests to do so. The myth of success and action from training delivered on time is maintained. Do you want to be part of that myth or do you want to be involved in solutions that really make a difference?

This is a classic case of quick-fix problem solving. The good thing about this process is that it is fast. The only problem is that it may not be fixing the problem at all. Peter Senge says that most of the problems that we are fixing today are yesterday's problems that have come back to haunt us.

why do line managers need to be skilled in performance analysis?

With the decline of intermediaries, line training officers and HR staff, the line manager is taking on more and more accountability for the performance of his or her people.

It is no longer adequate for a manager to be a subject-matter expert or a solo high performer. The manager of today has to be a coach and facilitator of high performance from his or her team.

what abilities do you need to be a successful performance coach?

- A high performer in the process that your team delivers.
- A role model of the beliefs, values and behaviours that your organisation expects.
- Interpersonal skills to build credibility with employees.
- Confidence and credibility to stand up to solutioneering and avoidance.

- Analytical ability to follow a systematic process to analyse needs.
- Creativity to synthesise appropriate solutions.
- Interpersonal skills to coach your employees.
- Bravery to give honest feedback.
- Perseverance to see things through.

Quite a list! This book is primarily about a process that you can use to improve employee performance. How successful you are in using it will depend on some of the 'softer' skills and attributes above. It will show you how to use a systematic process to analyse the real reasons behind performance problems. By working in partnership with your people you should be able to generate some real success stories and improve your skills and confidence.

some relevant theory

Many people have worked on performance analysis. The leaders in the field were **Robert Mager** and **Peter Pipe**, who published *Analysing Performance Problems* in 1984. Their approach involved analysing performance discrepancies (defined as the difference between people's actual performance and the performance desired) in terms of skill, motivation and other factors.

In 1981, **Peter Block** published *Flawless Consulting*, which dealt with wider issues such as 'contracting', 'understanding resistance', 'getting the data' and 'managing the feedback meeting'. Block stresses the need for consultants and managers to be authentic at all stages in the process, which he defines as:

1. Defining the initial problem.
2. Deciding to proceed with the project.
3. Selecting the dimensions to be studied.

4. Who is involved in the study?
5. Selecting the method.
6. Data collection.
7. Funnelling the data.
8. Data summary.
9. Data analysis.
10. Feedback of results.
11. Recommendations.
12. Decision on actions.

(Source: P Block, *Flawless Consulting*, 1981.)

Robinson and **Robinson** suggest that less than 30 per cent of what people learn is applied and that for learning to be effective the business, performance, learning and work environment needs must be defined and aligned. Their approach has three main stages: PARTNERSHIP – ASSESSMENT – IMPLEMENTATION:

PARTNERSHIP

a. Identify and Partner with Client(s)
b. Proactively identify Business Goals and Performance Initiatives
c. Respond to requests for Assistance
d. Conduct Initial Project Meeting(s)

ASSESSMENT

e. Agree upon Desired Performance
f. Determine Performance Strengths and Gaps
g. Determine Causes for Performance Problems
h. Report Results to Client(s); Agree on actions

IMPLEMENTATION

i. Partner with Client(s) to Implement Actions
j. Measure and report Results to Client(s)

(Copyright 1997 Partners in Change, Inc.)

Richard Beckhard developed a formula for organisational change that I have found invaluable:

For change to occur there must be:

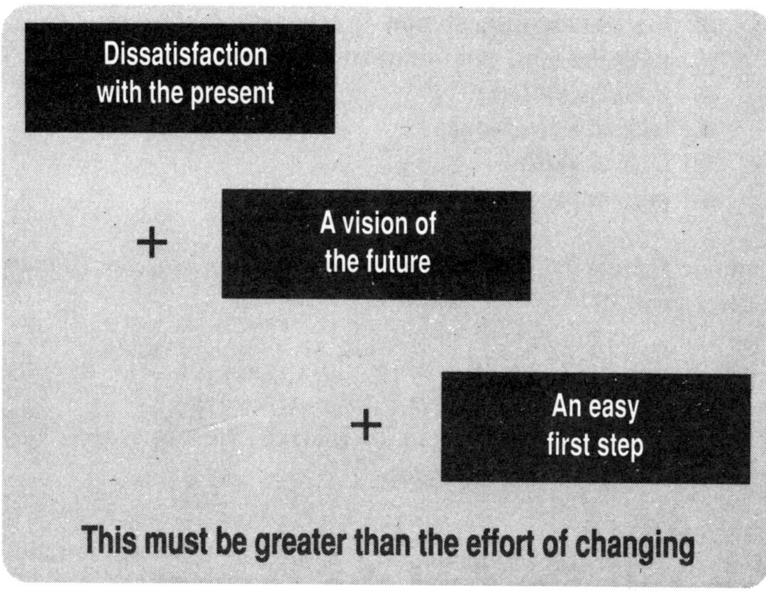

This is a very useful guideline for any change initiative, report, meeting etc. The seven-step process actually follows this change formula.

The main factors that affect a person's performance are:

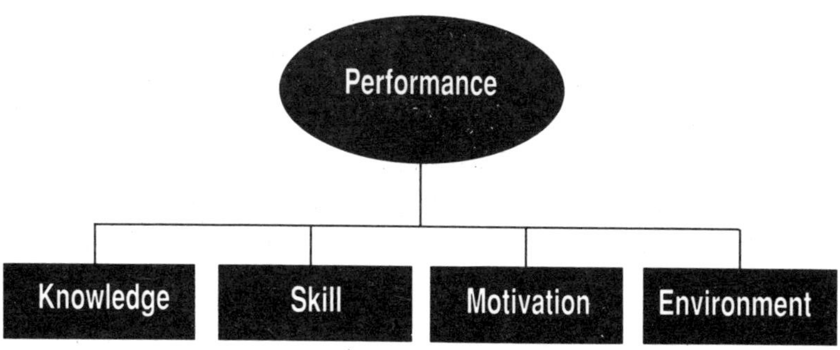

In 1978, **Thomas Gilbert** found that the reasons that people do not perform are caused by a combination of things, usually in this order:

- inadequate information or reference material;
- poor working environment or inadequate tools;
- poor incentives;
- lack of knowledge;
- lack of skill;
- poor motivation.

(Source: Thomas F Gilbert's Behaviour Engineering Model in *Human Competence*, 1978.)

Notice that most people want to do a good job. The reasons are usually very clear when you do some analysis.

Using the information from an analysis, we can analyse the reason for any performance gap.

how do we find the correct solutions?

It is very simple. We do not need to strive to create solutions. When we know the reasons for a gap, the solutions will be the opposite. Thus:

- if employees are not achieving targets because they do not know what is expected of them and have inadequate equipment to do the job,
- the solutions are to make the expectations clear and get them some new equipment!

example

I was once asked to design some training for a set of supervisors in a mail sorting office. The senior managers thought that they needed 'leadership' training. When I asked them about this they said things like: 'they lack fire in their belly', 'people never get back from breaks on time', 'they don't have control over the staff'.

When I talked to some supervisors I found that:

- they had all been promoted from small receiving offices into this large sorting office;
- they were promoted on seniority and time in the job;
- they had had no training in how to be a supervisor – it was assumed that because they had been promoted they could do the job;
- the sorting office was on four floors and covered a large area;
- the teams were highly unionised and had been doing the tasks for a long time;
- each supervisor was supposed to look after a team that worked on two levels and at seven different locations;
- the supervisors had an office in the corner of one level and no mobile phones;
- the sorting equipment was causing breakage, which took staff resources from the main team;
- they had no clear objectives.

No wonder they were not reaching their targets! We did not do any leadership training; instead my report forced a review of the management support for supervisors.

some change theory

It is also useful to realise that people react to change in a similar way. The classic reaction is:

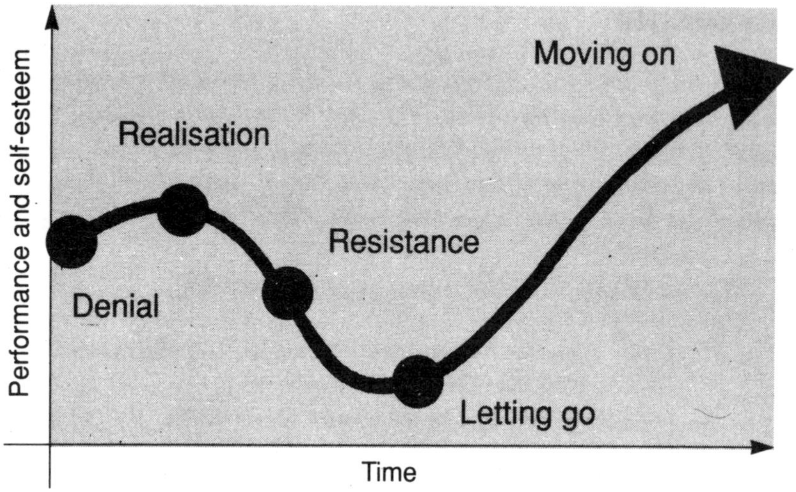

the change cycle

Many people do not realise that individuals and teams can move forward and backwards through this change cycle. In an organisation the common themes are:

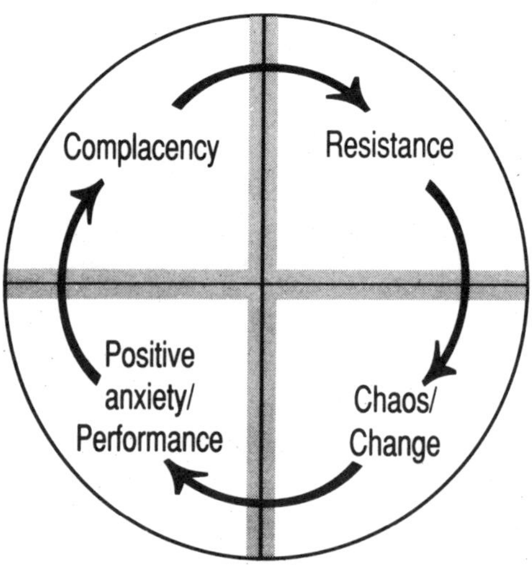

some principles

- You progress through the cycle in a clockwise direction.
- You can move backwards as well as forwards.
- You do not have to spend the same amount of time in each phase.
- You do not have to progress from one phase to another.
- There is no destination.
- You continue moving around the cycle for ever!

Where are you in this cycle? Where is your team? Where are individuals in your team? Where is your organisation? Try putting your people on the diagram. What you do with each person will depend on where they are in the cycle.

in complacency

- You may need to disturb people.
- Identify the problems.
- Identify the cost of the performance gap.
- Make things appear worse!
- Make them see that they cannot stay here.

in resistance

Usually categorised by denial: 'It is not our problem.'

- Make it clear that it is our problem.
- These are the people involved.
- We are part of the problem.
- We/you are on the diagram.

in chaos and change

- Provide a vision of where we want to be.
- Involve people in the solutions.
- Prioritise.
- Agree goals.
- Set action plans.

in positive anxiety/performance

I include this wonderful term 'positive anxiety' because effective teams are not complacent; they have a buzz about them, and they are often dissatisfied with their performance, even though they may be the best. When you are performing, the most important thing is to stop slippage into complacency, so:

- Set stretching new goals.
- Give regular feedback.
- Celebrate successes.
- Encourage and stimulate greater efforts.

self-image theory

One of the most powerful things that drives our behaviour is our self-image. Our unconscious mind makes us interact with the world around us to reinforce our image of ourselves. Thus someone who believes that they are lucky will see examples of their good fortune all around them and vice versa.

Mistakes and errors can be signs that a person does not feel comfortable in that role or job. They will not realise it but their creative subconscious will be making them act in a certain way. How we value ourselves and how we perform is dependent on our self-image and the comfort zone that matches this picture. In order to change behaviour, employees need to believe that they can change and visualise themselves achieving the desired performance. The stronger and more emotive the positive picture, the better chance of success.

We think in three dimensions:

- words;
- pictures;
- emotions.

The stronger the goal or success picture that you can share with your employees, the more likely they are to achieve it.

When we come to Step 4 in the process, 'What do we want people to do?', the most effective managers inspire their people with positive, emotional goals rather than activities.

an example

Let's plan to improve the performance of a cashier. Which group of phases is most likely to help?

- Not again, Frank!
- You always forget to ask the customer their date of birth.
- Your performance is not good enough.
- You don't look smart enough to go out to the front office.
- Why are we always having these talks?

or

- Frank, these mistakes are not like you.
- Try to guess how old each customer is – it might help you remember to ask his or her date of birth.
- I put you on the front counter because I have faith in you.
- You looked very smart on Monday – keep up that level of appearance.

Is that it? We have looked at a useful snapshot of the psychology of human behaviour and performance. The theory above has to be incomplete, but it might be just enough to help a line manager do something about understanding and improving their employees' performance.

why is this theory useful?

It means that we can analyse all the reasons for a given performance gap and find appropriate solutions. It does not matter that this analysis may not be perfect. It is better than no analysis at all.

The seven-step process is very simple but it is also a sophisticated change formula:

- We concentrate on people.
- We help them confront the reality of where they are now.
- We disturb them enough to realise that they cannot stay where they are.
- We build up a picture of where they could be.
- We get them to commit to some easy first steps in an action plan that includes names and dates.

It is a simple change formula that also is the basis of the sales process:

'Looking for a new car, sir?'
'Is that just for you or do you have a family?'
'Yes, I can see that the one you have now will be too small for all that baby stuff.'
'This model is still very sporty but the hatchback gives it plenty of room for push chairs, nappies, carry cots, toys etc.'
'It's on special offer this month and I could give you a very good price on your sports car.'

what about different types of performance gap?

Employees' performance problems can take place at many levels:

- individual;
- team;
- organisation.

Even at an individual level the problem involves several people. People never perform in isolation. The other great myth is that any performance problem 'is their problem'; if you are trying to raise 'their' performance then you are probably involved as well as several others.

You can use the same process to tackle a problem with your accounts team as you do with your mother-in-law! We will start with simpler examples and work up to more complex ones.

a seven-step process

There are several problem-solving processes. We have distilled these to a simple seven-step process, shown on page 24.

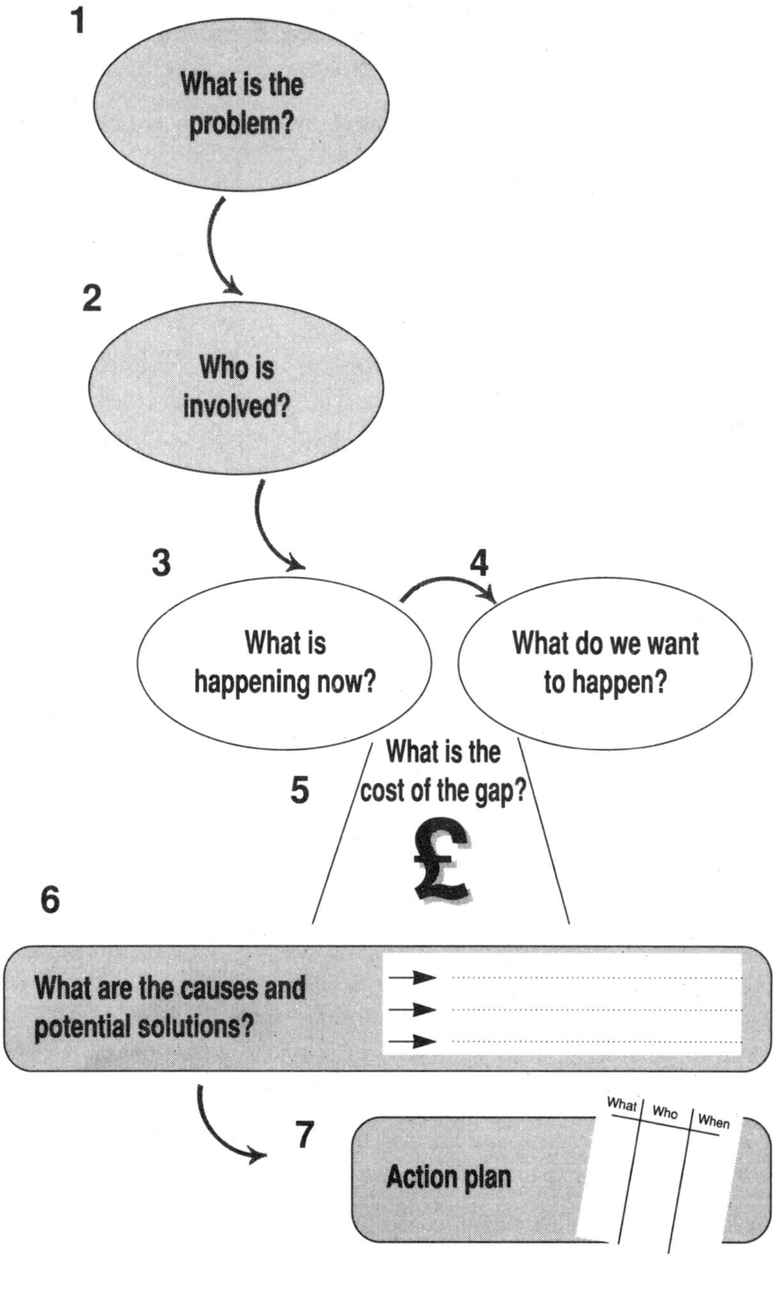
1
What is the problem?
2
Who is involved?
3
What is happening now?
4
What do we want to happen?
5
What is the cost of the gap?
£
6
What are the causes and potential solutions?
7
Action plan
What
Who
When

how can I use the process?

With this theory and process you can start to analyse any gap in employees' performance, whether it be to help them perform even better or to help them overcome a performance problem. You can use it:

- On your own, to analyse your own problems or problems with your employees.
- With someone else, your boss or a member of your team. When we are talking of such a meeting we will call the other person the 'client' whilst you are acting as the manager of a performance improvement process.
- In a group or team, as a group performance improvement process.

This book is written for line managers who need to improve their employees' performance either by working through the process on their own or with colleagues.

3

a simple example

how to improve Mike's fitness

Imagine that Mike is one of your staff who wants to improve his fitness. Manager One, in the Introduction, would probably just say: 'Go and join a gym, Mike!' Manager Two, on the other hand, takes some time to ask Mike a few questions and really get to the bottom of the problem and produce real solutions that are more likely to work.

As Mike describes it, the problem to be solved is how to get that daily run in every day. Using the seven-step process, the first thing is to find out is who is involved, apart from Mike.

who is involved?

In fact Mike identifies five key people:

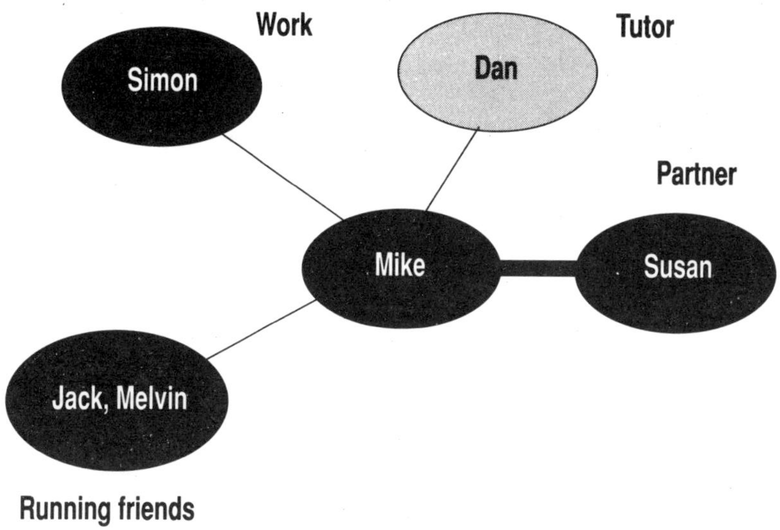

so, Mike, what is happening now?

- 'I haven't got time to go running.'
- 'Work and studying get greater priority.'
- 'I run when I am at home, once a week, which I don't find acceptable.'
- 'I run alone (not by choice).'
- 'Susan does not run.'

what do you want to be able to do?

- 'I would like to do a run every day!'
- 'But I would be satisfied by three times a week.'

how big would you say this gap is?

- 'I feel a minor level of frustration.'
- 'I miss out on having a healthy body and healthy mind.'
- 'Running helps me focus on my studying.'

is the cost of this gap serious?

- 'Yes, I want to do something about it!'

can we identify the causes for the gap and some possible solutions?

'Perhaps I need help in my time management.'

can we make the performance easier in any way?

'Yes, I can aim for 3 times per week instead of every day.'

can you use a checklist?

'Yes, I will mark mornings on the calendar when I can run and when I do run.'

did you once run every day?

'Yes I used to run with Jack and Melvin. I could try to find people at work who want to run at lunchtime.'

I wonder if your goal of every day is realistic?	*Three days a week is more realistic*
Do you have sufficient performance feedback?	*Not at the moment; I will keep a chart of my times*
If you do more running do you suffer in any way?	*No, if I run I feel better able to handle the work and my course. Every day takes a lot of time though. I will reward myself for achieving my running targets*
If you do not go for a run do you benefit in any way?	*Yes, if I do not go for a run I can have dinner with Susan. I will ask Susan if she doesn't mind eating dinner later so I can fit in a run*
Does it really matter to you?	*Yes it does, I will find a club and run with colleagues*
Can you make it mean even more?	*I could take up fell running? Find out about orienteering?*
Do you fear failure?	*Yes, every day is too much. I will be realistic and do what I can*
Is there anything wrong with your environment, methods and equipment?	*Yes, I need some new shoes and a running watch plus a calendar to record my times*

Are the 'managers' playing their part in helping you to perform?	*I will ask Susan to support me and promise a meal out when I reach my study and running targets*
Are there any other obstacles stopping you?	*There are no showers at work, I will see if we can arrange something*
So what are you doing to do then, Mike?	*Fell running is not convenient*
And when are you going to do it?	*I will start tonight before I start studying*

What	Who	When
The new shoes will have to wait until pay day	*Me*	*Next month*
I will talk to Susan tonight and set up the calendar	*Susan and me*	*Tonight*
I will find out about joining a club with some colleagues from work	*See Jim*	*This lunchtime*
I will start before I start studying	*Me*	*Tonight*

what happened when we analysed Mike's problem?

1. We looked at who was involved.
2. We looked at what is happening now.
3. We looked at what he wants to happen.
4. We checked that the gap was worth doing something about:
   - Is the cost of this gap serious?
   - 'Yes, I want to do something about it.'
5. We investigated the possible reasons why Mike is finding it hard to get that run in every day:
   - knowledge;
   - skills;
   - motivation; and
   - environment.
6. These questions raised a number of possible solutions.
7. We discarded the fell running as impractical and combined the others into an action plan.

Easy, isn't it?

lessons from the running example

Are you surprised at just what is involved in really understanding how to get that run in?

First, the problem was not running every day. The hope to run every day was one of the unrealistic goals that was stopping Mike – however, it emerged that cutting down was a solution, not the problem. By working through his performance gap and all the causes, we came up with a range of solutions. Put them all together with an action plan with dates on it and

Mike might actually start running again. Many of the factors were motivational and environmental. But they are mixed up. I hope you can see the need for a systematic approach to analysing what is going on.

- Problems never involve only one person; they always involve the interaction of people within a system.
- Solutions to performance problems are often not radical. You may just need time to think it through logically.
- Solutions are usually found as groups of actions rather than one big, magic solution.
- Often the assumed problem is not the real problem at all.
- Facing up to your problems is the first step to solving them.

What lessons did you learn from the example? Ready to try it yourself?

4

the seven-step performance improvement process

'Nothing is more useful than a good process.'

the process

Analysing performance problems and designing solutions can be simplified into seven steps:

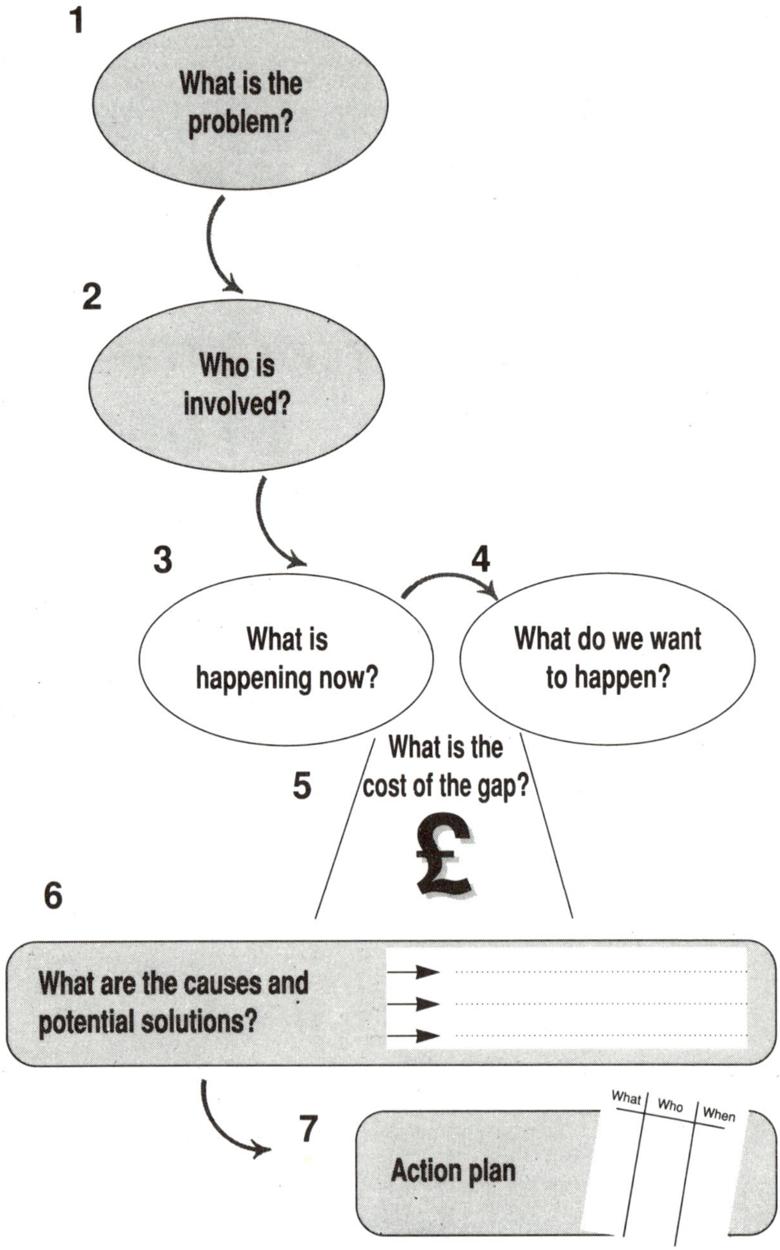
1
What is the problem?
2
Who is involved?
3
What is happening now?
4
What do we want to happen?
5
What is the cost of the gap?
£
6
What are the causes and potential solutions?
7
Action plan
What
Who
When

To get started, use the checklist on the next few pages. It contains all the prompts that you need.

think of a problem that you have right now

This is an opportunity to get some immediate value from the process. Choose a relatively simple personal issue, such as 'How do I...

- keep fit?'
- make more time for my family?'
- get the builders to finish the extension?'
- cope with my in-laws this weekend?'

Now answer the questions in the checklist to analyse the causes of your performance gap and find some solutions. It is important that you do this for real – fetch a piece of paper or write on this book. If you are worried about keeping a clean copy, why not stick Post-its on the blank sections and write on them? You also have my permission to photocopy and reuse the checklist for your own use.

a checklist

step 1 – what is the problem?

- Not the assumed solution!
- What is the real problem?

step 2 – who is involved?

- Draw a diagram of all the people involved in the problem.

- Put the key people in the centre.
- Make links between the key people.
- Label what is happening between them.

step 3 – what is happening now?

- Describe what is happening now.
- What are the key people doing now?
- Try to get facts, figures, anything measurable.

step 4 – what do we want to happen?

- Visualise how you would like things to be.
- How will you know when you have reached this state?
- Try to visualise a strong picture of what success looks like.

step 5 – what is the cost of the gap?

- What would happen if you did nothing?
- Estimate the cost of the gap if it were to remain.
- If you cannot find a serious gap then consider leaving things alone!

step 6 – what are the causes and potential solutions?

- Try to generate as many solutions as possible. Suspend judgement as to their feasibility, and put them all down in the right-hand column.

have they got the required knowledge and skills?

Think about the key player or players who affect the performance gap.

Question	Potential Solution
Do you think they lack some knowledge or skill?	Can we make the performance easier in any way? (Simplify the tasks? Split the job? Design checklists? Clarify performance standards?)
Were they once able to do it?	Try practice, better information, and performance feedback.
Have they got the capability to learn to do this?	Consider training them or providing learning materials.
If they haven't got the capability to learn to do this	Can we transfer them to a job that they can do? Or terminate their employment?

motivation

Question	Potential Solution
Do they get poor feedback on positive as well as negative performance?	Provide clear goals and regular feedback on positive as well as negative performance.
If they do it right, do they suffer in any way, eg by being given more work?	Reduce the punishment for high performance. Introduce rewards and incentives.
Are they being rewarded for low performance?	Stop the rewards.
Do people lack self-esteem?	Help them visualise success, set positive goals. Catch people doing things right, build on success.

environment

Question	Potential Solution
Is there anything wrong with their environment, methods, equipment?	Improve.
Are the managers helping?	Improve management.
Any other obstacles?	Try to remove them.

step 7 – action plan

Look at the list of possible solutions in the right-hand column.

Cross out those:

- that are just not feasible;
- whose cost would be greater than the benefit.

Highlight those:

- that can be easily implemented;
- that will give the best results for minimum effort.

Of those that are left, can you combine them into things that go together?

Now agree in which order to do things. Make an action plan of the solutions you are going to try.

What	Who	When

'It's Magic'

An example of using the checklist to raise the performance of a magic act.

step 1 – what is the problem?

Mandy is part of a magic act called 'It's Magic', led by David. She is worried about David's performance:

'David is too laid back and naive about stagework and set in his ways. I am the only one to question everything; lately he is standing up to me (which is good) but he doesn't really listen to what I have to say.'

step 2 – who is involved?

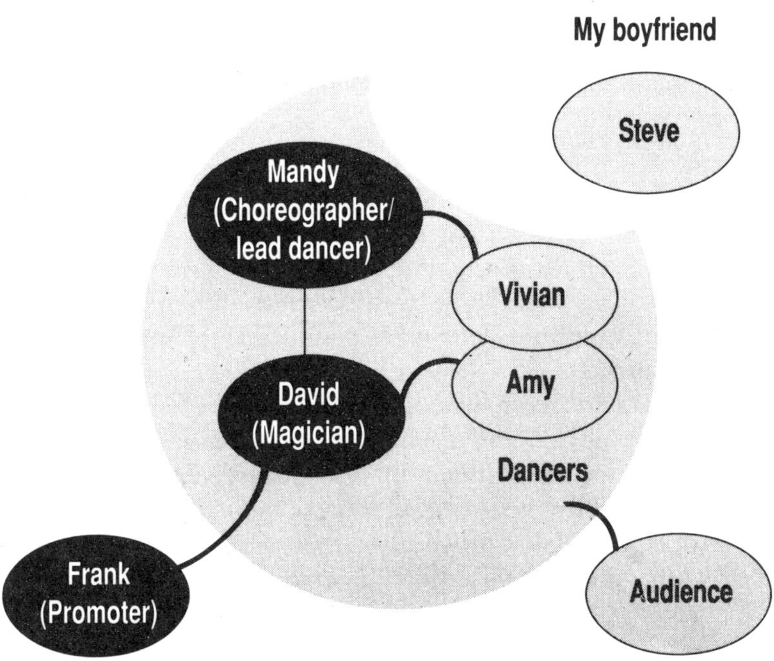

step 3 – what is happening now?

'"Its Magic" has been going for 18 months. We have a 30-minute act, which we perform in small halls, at Christmas mainly, to audiences of 100–150. We make no money but just cover our costs. We are all employed elsewhere and do it as a hobby.

'David is agreeing to my advice but then not taking it. He is still relying on me when it all goes wrong. I am concerned that we do not rehearse enough. He is 19 years old and works in a bank and is bored at work; he likes to try difficult tricks and would like to turn professional.

'I have a busy job in insurance. I am 29 years old, don't want to work in an unprofessional act and want some of my spare time back. Vivian and Amy are both 19 and work in banks; they do not contribute their ideas and opinions enough. It all seems to get left to me.

'David has been approached by an agent and has agreed to do a one-hour audition for a big show. I know that we do not have enough material for this. David has said yes but we have not discussed it.'

step 4 – what do we want to happen?

'I can either quit the group with no hard feelings, knowing they are going to carry on okay, or we continue with me taking less responsibility, and I'd have more confidence in David and the group's future.

'I want David to rely less on me and take the helm properly. To heed my advice and become more conscious of the end result, take more care of detail. I also want Vivian and Amy to respond and input their ideas more.

'If we continue, I want to play similar-sized venues, but fill them with a good-quality show of about 40 minutes.'

step 5 – what is the cost of the gap?

'If we do nothing we could end up disappointing our next audience with a poor-quality show. David and I will possibly come to blows, I may leave, the group will fail and David will never be successful professionally. I will feel guilty and could be blamed for the break-up.

'In my opinion, it is worth doing something about the potential loss of good friends, 18 months' hard work and my professionalism. I want to do something about it, but what?'

'Is the cost of the gap serious?'

'Yes.'

step 6 – what are the causes and potential solutions?

Question	Potential Solution
Do you think David lacks some knowledge or skill?	David does not know what goes into a successful show.
Can we make the performance easier in any way?	Simplify the tasks? Split the job? Design checklists? We could get a manager. Clarify his magician performance standards and give him a checklist for rehearsals and before the first show.
Was David once able to do the show?	No, I don't think he has ever been good at detail. But he can do good shows when I manage him.
Do you do it often?	(Try practice, better information, and performance feedback.) We need more rehearsal.

Has he got the capability to learn how to do this?	Yes. Consider training him or providing learning materials. I might buy him an autobiography of a great magician. He could also go to magic school.
If they haven't got the capability to learn to do this.	Can we transfer them to a job that they can do? Can we terminate their employment?

motivation

Does David get poor feedback on performance?	His parents and friends tell him he is great. No one gives constructive criticism after the act. I could get an experienced magician to come and give us some feedback. Provide clear goals and regular feedback on positive as well as negative performance. We need to rehearse three times as much as now.
If they do it right, do they suffer in any way, eg by being given more work?	Yes, I cover up for him and it all comes right on the night. I will have to be more assertive, give him a checklist of what needs to be done and risk him not doing it. Reduce the punishment for high performance. I think this audition matters to him but he doesn't realise what

	is involved. I will have to talk to him about how serious he is about going professional. Introduce rewards and incentives. Make rewards based on performance.
Is he being rewarded for low performance?	Yes, David gets positive feedback whatever happens. Stop the rewards for low performance.
Do people lack self-esteem?	Probably – we will have to confront our weakness and strengths as a group and see how we can support each other. Help them visualise success, set positive goals. Catch people doing things right, build on success.

environment

Is there anything wrong with their environment, methods, equipment?	Yes, the big magic tricks have to be collapsible because we only have a small van.
Are the managers helping?	What managers?! Perhaps that is what we need. I am doing it all. Improve management.
Any other obstacles?	This audition is a threat; we need to get together to discuss it. I am convinced that we have not got enough stuff.

Try to remove them. Perhaps we could ask the agent to our next show and concentrate on getting that right and pull out of the audition. We could have a stronger identity; we ought to agree where we are going and get some new costumes.

can we combine these things?

- I could borrow my brother's big van for the next show. Then we could work on bettering the tricks – building sturdier, more fail-safe structures.
- Perhaps we could ask the agent to our next show and concentrate on getting that right and pull out of the audition.
- We could agree with David to really get the act together so we can impress his agent and help his chances of going professional.
- I'll find out about magic school for David and buy him that biography.
- We can develop a checklist. Do we feel absolutely confident with performance of tricks, ie done 10 times with no problems – checked stage for angles, etc. Music ready – done a video recording to check and give ourselves feedback, etc.
- Make it matter to David, get honest feedback from family and friends.
- If this doesn't work, suggest David goes solo and gets a different agent.

step 7 – action plan

What	Who	When
Arrange a meeting of the group	*All of us*	*Next Wednesday*
Plan agenda, buy book, research magic school, arrange to borrow van	*Me*	*Before next Wednesday*
Design checklist	*All*	*Before next rehearsal*

lessons from 'It's Magic'

The issues in the magic act are not too different from a business team:

- People perform as part of a system.
- Performance depends on the interaction of different people in a system.
- To understand the reason for low performance in a group you need to understand the relationships between the people and their individual motivations.
- It is essential to draw a diagram to get the relationships out in the open. Then you can concentrate on analysing the reason for poor performance, in different parts of the diagram.
- The solutions are a mixture of environment, knowledge and information; there is no 'magic' single solution.

Now that you have seen the process in outline and some examples, we will look at each step in more detail.

5

step 1 – what is the problem?

how to deal with 'solutioneering'

The first step in following the seven-step process is to focus on an initial idea of the problem and to avoid the solutioneering start. You may have unwittingly thought of the solution before you have understood the problem.

Other people often present problems to you as solutions. Imagine your boss in the following scenario:

Director: Glad you could come in, Jack, we need some prices and a delivery date to run some project-management training. How soon can you get that to me?

Be careful here! Your boss will probably be very pleased that he or she has a solution in mind and will have some enthusiasm and personal emotion attached to it, so do *not* say: 'Hang on a minute! Training is a solution, I want to know what the problem is first!'

When faced with a solutioneering start, it is important to go along with the energy of your client and use it to your advantage. Try to get the focus straight away on to who is involved in this problem rather than the solution, eg:

Manager: You want it for all project managers? Are there any in particular who are having problems?

The conversation might continue:

Director: Virtually all new product launches are running six months behind schedule!
Manager: Who is involved in new product launches?
Director: The marketing product managers are the key ones.

define the apparent problem

I would go along with the assumption that someone needs some project-management training, but at some stage I might clarify the perceived or presenting problem:

Manager: So the problem seems to be new product launches being six months behind schedule?
Director: Yes, and they are 20 per cent over budget.
Manager: So the problem is that new products are being launched six months late and 20 per cent over budget?
Director: Yes, that's why we need some project management training pretty urgently!

Ignore the last statement, roll with it for the time being but focus on the problem.

the presenting problem

Doctors will talk about:

- presenting problems;
- symptoms;
- diagnosis;
- causes;
- treatment.

That is because they are trained to use a process of diagnostic problem solving. Imagine if they adopted the quick-fix solution approach:

Doctor: Good morning Mr Smith, how are you?
Patient: Not very well I am afraid, Doctor.
Doctor: Well, how about some Valium, that should make you feel better.
Patient: Yes, but what about fixing my broken ankle!

As managers, we need to behave like doctors. We will be presented with an apparent problem. It is our job not to jump to conclusions but to diagnose the causes of the problem. Doctors call the initial apparent problem the presenting problem. This can be a useful term to help us distinguish between the apparent problem and the real problem.

For example, the presenting problem in an organisation could be low profits, whereas this is really a symptom of the problem, which could be a number of things:

- bad weather;
- high wastage;
- low sales.

examples of 'solutioneering'

Once you become sensitive to solutioneering you will start to hear it everywhere:

'You need a new lawnmower, that one sounds clapped out.'
'I think we need more parking spaces.'
'We need to get rid of him, he is hopeless.'
'I need some training.'
'You need some training.'
'I need to improve my sales figures.'
'I need to join Weight Watchers.'
'Keep your head still when you swing.'
'This dehumidifier will reduce condensation.'

Let's have another look at these statements:

'Lawnmower sounds rough.'
'Yes, I put the wrong petrol in it.'
'I think we need more parking spaces.'
'More people could take the bus to work, you mean.'
'He is hopeless.'
'Well, you recruited him and he was fine in his last job.'
'I need some training.'
'Are you sure that you know what we expect from you?'
'You need some training.'
'I have not got time to spend coaching you.'
'I need to improve my sales figures.'
'Your conversion rate is high, you just need more appointments.'
'I need to lose weight so I am going to join Weight Watchers.'
'Why not just change your self-image to a healthy eating person and see what happens?'
'Keep your head still when you swing.'
'Watch the ball.'
'This dehumidifier will reduce condensation.'
'Open your windows.'

Conversations are often a mixture of assumed problems, solutions and opinions. This is fine as a pastime, but a line manager cannot afford to use the same process for managing employee performance. Otherwise, they will spend a large proportion of their time and emotional energy continually fixing and re-fixing.

'Boss, he is back from the training course and nothing has improved. Can we send him on another one?'

'Well, I tried to sack him and he said that he had never had clear expectations in the role and was taking us to a tribunal.'

'I bought the new lawnmower that you suggested and it is as bad as the old one; it seems that we were using the wrong petrol.'

'We need more parking spaces, everyone says they should be able to drive to work.'

So break out of the cycle! Use a simple diagnostic problem-solving process to find out the causes for some of your everyday employee problems and find some more permanent solutions. What have you got to lose?

be careful about how you specify the problem

Here are some examples of USAF pilots reporting problems to the maintenance crews for them to fix before the next flight and their replies!

'Number three engine missing.'
'Engine found on right wing after brief search.'

'Something loose in cockpit.'
'Something tightened in cockpit.'

'Left inside tyre almost needs replacement.'
'Almost replaced left inside main tyre.'

'Aircraft handles FUNNY.'
'Aircraft warned to straighten up, "fly right" and be serious.'

'Target radar hums.'
'Reprogrammed target radar with the words.'

(With thanks to Peter and Nick and the USAF ground crews.)

exercise

Please write down your answers on a piece of paper, or in the spaces provided.

Think of meetings that you have recently had. Can you think of any examples when you accepted an assumed solution rather than asking questions to understand the problem?

Plan how you will start off the next meeting you have. Write down what you intend to do.

be clear who your customer is

Who is the customer for your solution? It might be you. But in some cases you may be solving problems for your boss or the organisation. A good way to find out who your customers are is to think ahead to who will see the outputs of your work.

Manager: When I come back with my proposals, who will need to see them?

Director: Oh, I will have to get it passed by the Executive Committee.

Manager: What will they be interested in?

Director: Timescales; they want any solution to use up some of this year's budget. Any expenditure has to be invoiced before April.

So, a crucial step in finding out the problem is to identify your customer/s and any expectations that they might have.

Once you have a rough idea of the problem, whilst avoiding solutioneering, you are ready to start investigating the problem in more detail.

6

step 2 – who is involved?

why identify people at this stage?

Performance problems are about people. People often talk about a problem as if it is something to do with a thing like a computer application or a procedure. Computer applications and procedures do not have problems; it is always the people involved who have the problem and who will be part of the solution.

People never perform in isolation. In the simple example we saw that even Mike wanting to get his daily run involves other people. Problems at work always involve others.

To understand the reasons for performance problems, we need to draw a picture of all the people involved in the system.

what is a system diagram?

Let's take the simple example of Mike, who wants to solve the problem of how to get his run every day!

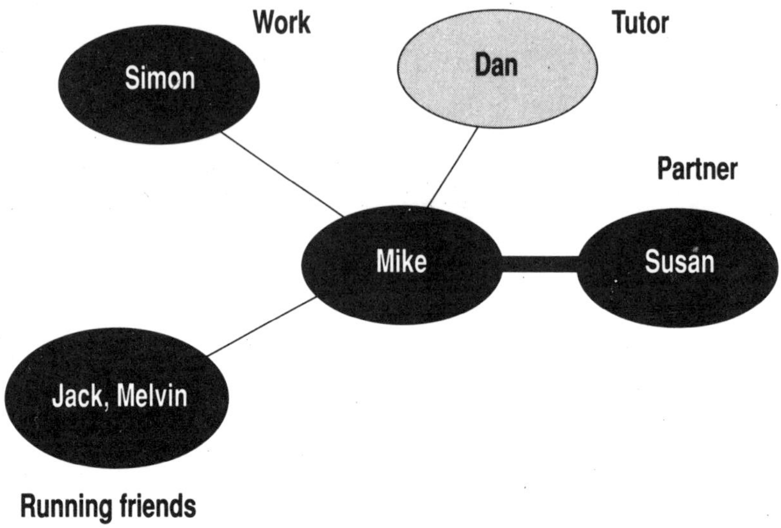

The lines show the interaction between people. You can draw a thick line for an important interaction and put the key players in the centre of the diagram.

some principles

- The person you are talking to should be on the diagram.
- The diagram can also describe the process.

System diagrams can also describe the process of a performance and any interaction with inanimate objects such as computer systems. Good questions to ask when drawing a system diagram are: 'What happens from the beginning, who is involved and what happens first?' or, 'If you stapled yourself to an order, what would you see as it moved through your organisation?'

put the customer on the diagram

A common mistake is to omit the customer from the diagram. Systems usually produce some output for the customer somewhere. In this case, Mike is the customer.

diagrams can make sense of complex situations

You will find that drawing a system diagram is a very powerful tool. The system diagram not only contains information about the people and relationships, but you can annotate the picture with performance information. I normally annotate the diagram with key phrases about what is going on between people.

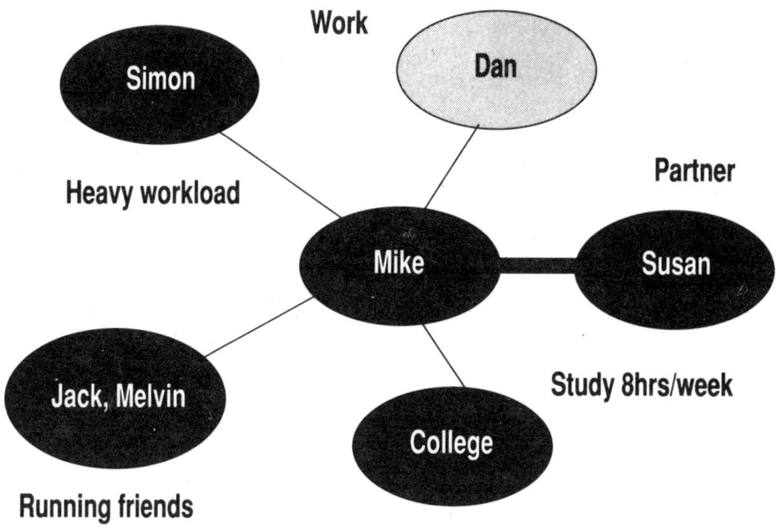

how do I draw a system diagram?

The first thing to do is to get a large piece of paper. If you are working on someone else's problem, put the paper between you.

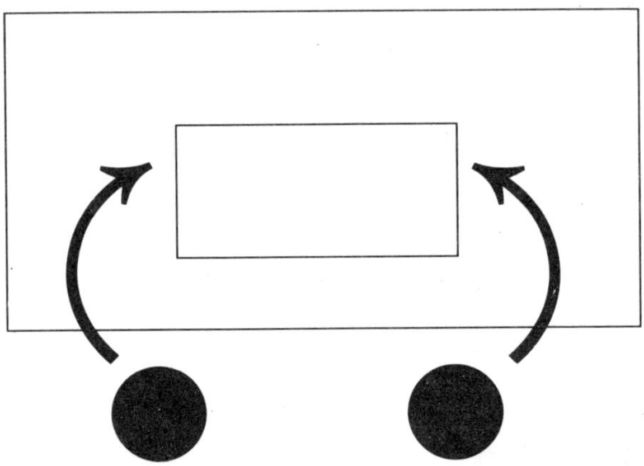

Then draw the key player or players in the centre of the paper, for example:

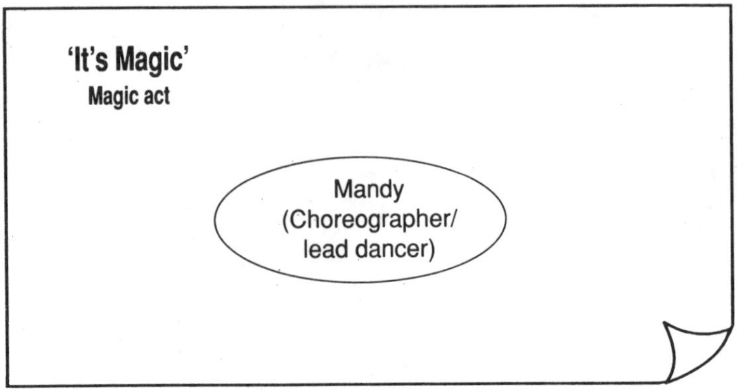

Consider who else is involved in the performance gap:

- Add these supporting players.
- Draw lines to illustrate interaction.
- You can draw thicker lines for significant relationships.

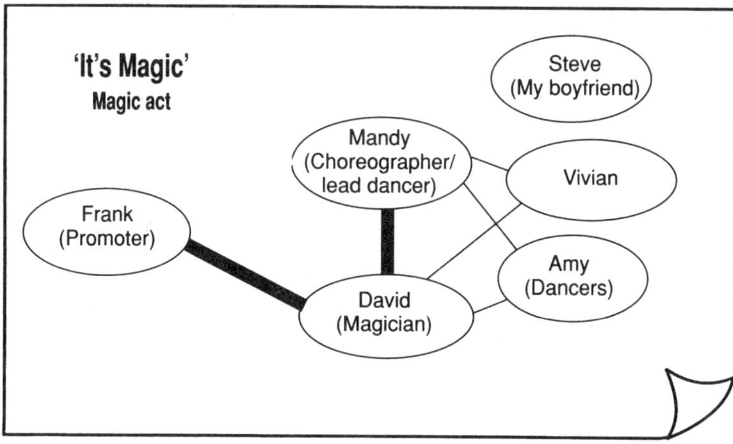

Finally:

- Draw a line around the key players who perform.
- A system usually produces some outputs, usually to a customer.
- Don't forget to put the customer on the diagram.

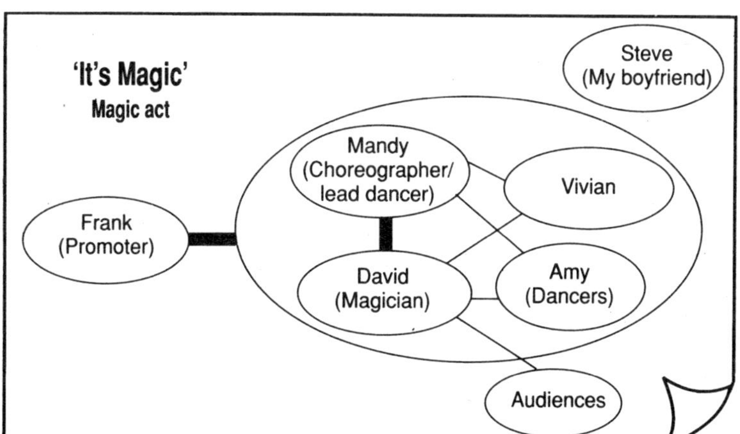

You can also label the interactions; what is happening between the key players:

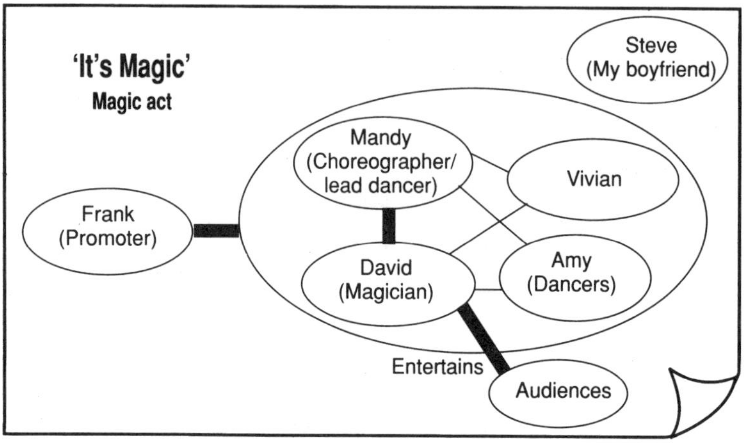

Some hints:

- Use a large piece of paper.
- Put the key player in the centre of the paper.
- Add the other players that are involved in the performance gap.
- Draw interactions as lines.
- Label these with actions if useful.
- Use thicker lines for greater interaction.
- Draw a line around the key players who perform.
- Don't forget to put the customer on the diagram.
- Use colour.

Have a look at the following example. Then try drawing a diagram for your problem.

example system diagram – a bank

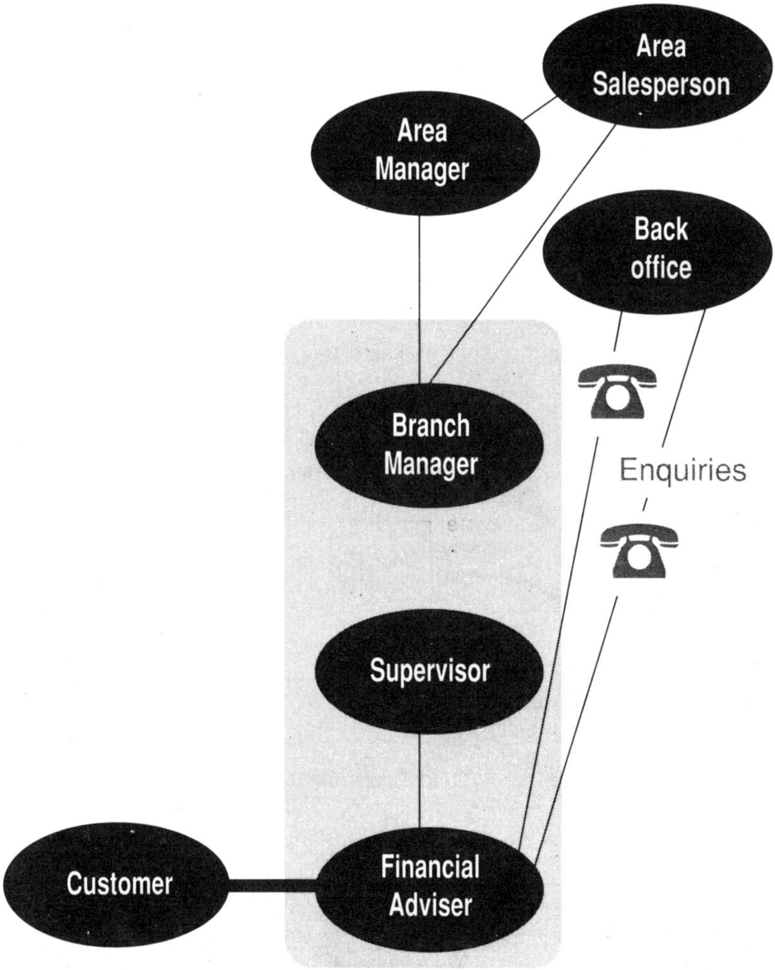

example system diagram – a training department

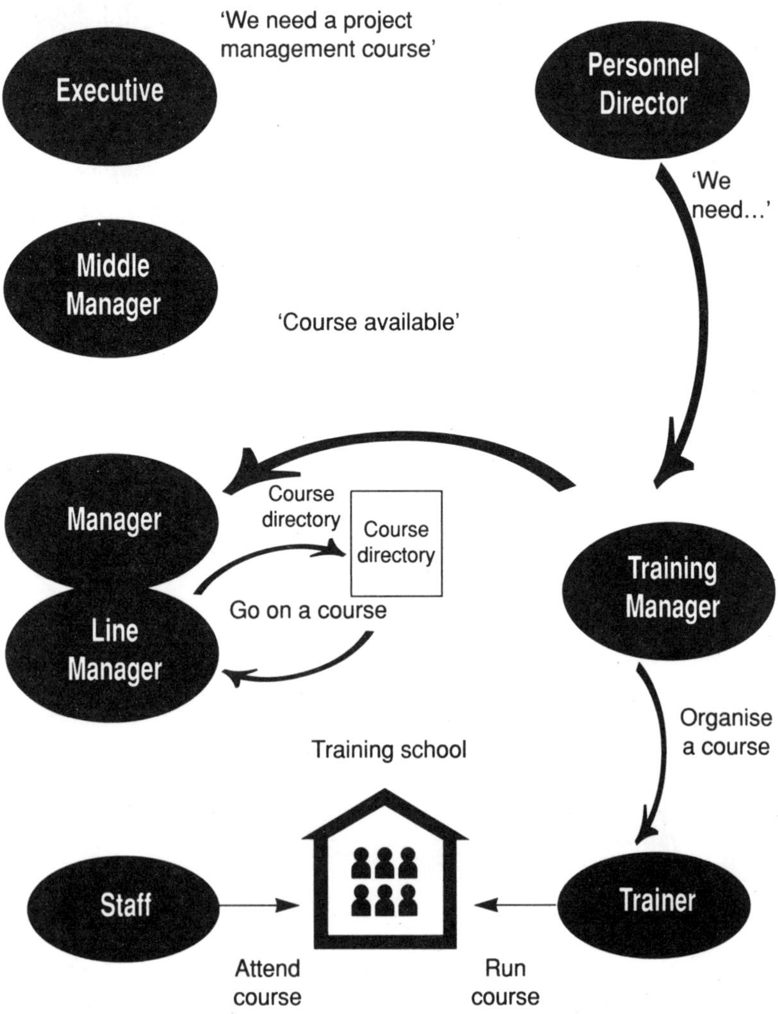

example system diagram – pension sales

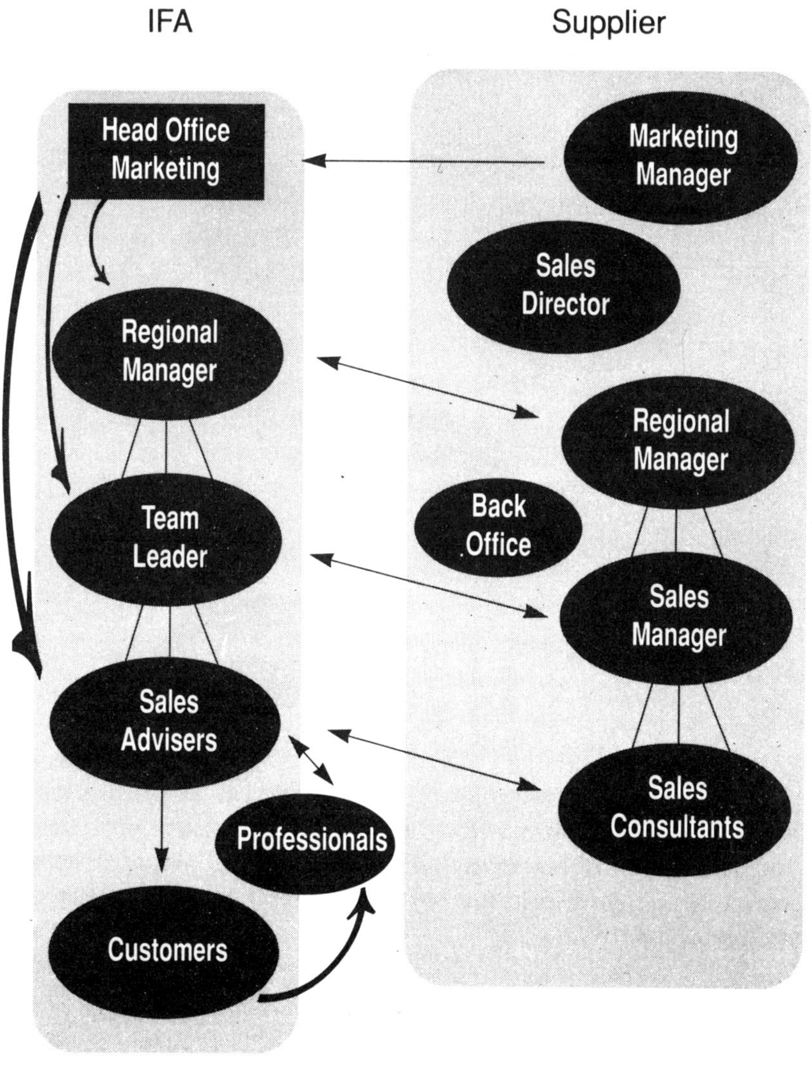

example system diagram – a charity

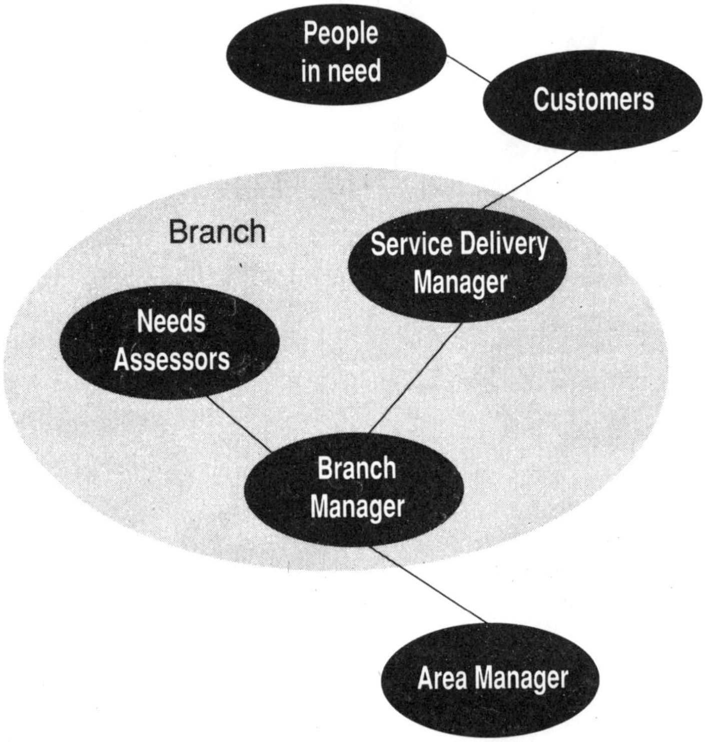

The first step of identifying who is involved can be much more than a start. By drawing a rich system diagram you can describe the problem visually on one sheet of paper. I have solved some problems just by drawing the system diagram, shown on page 63.

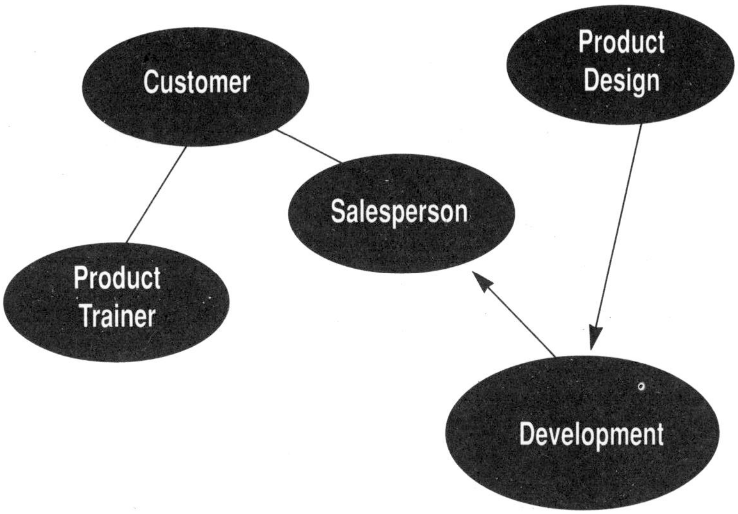

In this case there was no feedback loop from the customers or the product trainers into the product design!

Issues about improving performance are complex. The best way to handle complexity is to draw a diagram. Try it – it works.

Now we have a view of the presenting problem and a picture of the people and processes involved, we can move on to investigating what is really happening now.

7

step 3 – what is happening now?

what is a performance gap?

Gap analysis is a common technique used in sales and business planning. It is basically just comparing where people are now and where you want them to be.

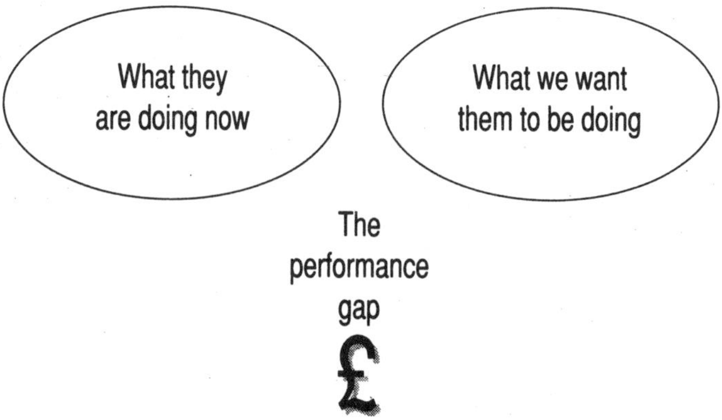

The power in performance analysis is that you also quantify the size of the gap. You should always try to get a financial value but also take notice of less measurable gaps, eg 'we will go out of business', 'a lot of unwanted stress' etc.

how to start defining what is happening now

In reality any problem will actually be made up of several performance gaps. So where do you start?

Let us imagine that you are a bank manager who has a problem with Anne, the number 1 cashier. The first assumption to be aware of is that the problem is probably not only with her. It will involve a combination of people within a 'system', which can be drawn on a diagram. You would probably draw the supervisor, colleagues and customers. In this case the system that performs is a branch.

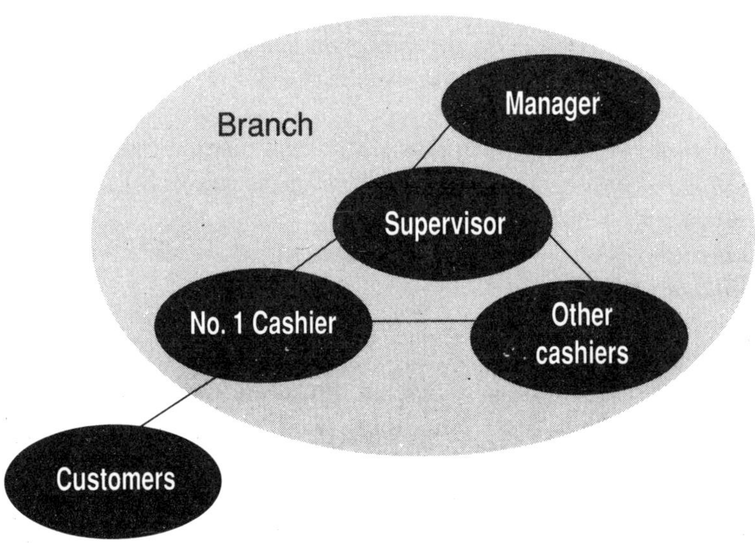

what is happening now?

number 1 cashier

Manager: 'How is cashier 1 performing now?'
'She got a 3 rating, which is excellent, on her performance review, but that is not the point. The problem is that she is over-performing; she brings in all the new business for the team.'

the system

The system that performs is the branch. The system will usually have performance measures already. So if the organisation already collects performance data at the level of branch, department or shop, this is what you want to find out.

Manager: 'How is the branch doing?'
'Profit and customer service are low.'

ask probing questions

To get to the bottom of the performance gap you need to ask probing questions to focus down on the detail. For example:

Question: 'What is your profitability and customer service?'
Manager: 'We are 10 per cent below target and score .5 on the Customer Service Index.'
Question: 'What is 10 per cent below target worth?'
Manager: '£200,000.'
Question: 'And what does .5 mean on customer service? What is the target?'
Manager: 'The target is .7. We are not doing well.'
Question: 'What does 'not doing well' mean in comparison with other branches?'
Manager: 'Second from bottom for the region.'

The principle is to keep asking until you get something that can be measured.

why is it so important to get measures about what is happening now?

The lack of a clear and quantified performance gap may be a major part of the problem. Identifying the problem may be the major step in solving it.

Some examples of getting a clearer idea about the gap:

- *'Lawnmower sounds rough, how long has it sounded like that?'*
  'Oh, since I filled it up with petrol.'
  'Which can did you use?'
  'The green one.'
- *'I think we need more parking spaces.'*
  'Why?'
  'On Monday a customer could not find a space.'
  'Why?'
  'There was a bus strike and everyone came by car. Some people parked in the customer spaces.'
- *'He is hopeless.'*
  'What do you mean by hopeless?'
  'His appearance is too scruffy for the front office.'
- *'I need some training.'*
  'Are you sure that you know what we expect from you?'
  'I assume it is to do X.'
  'No, it is to do two times X!'
- *'You need some training.'*
  'I know how to do it. It is just that I do not agree with the policy.'

- *'I need to improve my sales figures.'*
  'My conversion rate is high, I just need more appointments.'
- *'I need to lose weight so I am going to join Weight Watchers.'*
  'I eat too much junk food and snack between meals, and driving to work does not help.'
- *'Keep your head still when you swing.'*
  'You are looking up to see where the ball goes.'
- *'This dehumidifier will reduce condensation.'*
  'When did the problem start?'
  'When we had double glazing fitted.'

Asking questions about the existing performance is simply the first part of trying to quantify the size of the performance gap. Now we have some measures for the existing state, we can compare this with what we want to see.

step 4 – what do we want to happen?

creating a vision of the future

Once you have created a picture of the existing state, you can contrast this with a vision of the desired state. An easy way to do this is to use two columns. On one side you list the existing performances of each part of the system, eg:

Who	Doing Now	Want Them To Do
System (the branch)	20% below profit =£200k Customer Service Index .5 second from bottom	
Cashier 1	doing all new sales	
Customers	happy	
Other cashiers	no new sales	
Supervisor	not a proven seller	
Manager	worried that Anne might leave	

Once you have the list of how people are performing now, it is fairly simple to ask your client how they would like to see each part of the system perform, eg:

Who	Doing Now	Want Them To Do
System (the branch)	20% below profit = £200k	hit profit target
	Customer Service Index .5	Customer Service Index .7
	second from bottom	top half of league
Cashier 1	doing all new sales	helps others sell
Customers	happy	happy to buy from any cashier
Other cashiers	no new sales	all making an equal contribution
Supervisor	not a proven seller	helps Anne to coach the others
Manager	worried that Anne might leave	happy that all cashiers can sell
		achieve my bonus for an effective sales team

visualising the desired performance

You can see that having a clear existing state makes it much easier to identify what you want to see. Some questions that might help:

- 'What would it look like if things were going exactly as you would want them?'

- 'If you could imagine the ideal branch, what would people be doing?'
- 'Describe what it would look like in nine months' time if all these solutions have been successful.'
- 'What would you really like it to look like?'

using high performers

A very useful tactic in helping you to visualise what you want people to be able to do is to find someone who can do it already:

- 'What do they do?'
- 'How is it different from what people are doing now?'
- 'How did they learn to do it like that?'

If you cannot find any high performers in your organisation, can you identify any in another, perhaps in another sector? How do other companies always have enough parking spaces for visitors? What system do they use?

In a real example I interviewed the top insurance salesman in a company. The normal fact-find took 30 minutes to complete, too long for most customers. I found that he used to ask for a sheet of the customer's headed paper, then he asked the fact-find questions and wrote the answers on the headed paper.

The first five questions on the fact-find were about the company name, address and registered office etc. As these were already on the headed paper he saved time. He also got all fact-find answers on one sheet of paper so that it could be faxed for a quote by return. This was how he improved the process and won quick business. The other salespeople were just complaining about how long the fact-find took.

In another case I asked my golfing mother how she always holes out in two putts when she is on the green: ' I do not try to get the ball in the hole from my first putt, I just imagine that the hole is the size of a dustbin lid and try to get it in that.' Similarly, my squash improved significantly when a top player told me to imagine that there was a tree growing in the centre of the court. It was okay to hit the ball wherever there were no leaves!

High performers often naturally use visualisation tricks. This is the sort of thing you want to share with the rest of your employees.

motivating goals

People have a tendency to jump to solutions and actions too quickly. You can help bring about enduring change by setting goals rather than rushing to activity. For example, the manager in the cashier case might suddenly see some things that could help:

Manager: 'So if I made this a team target and gave some incentive and status for the No.1 cashier to coach the others, that would help.'

Well, obviously it is a good idea but these are actions, not goals. A goal is a powerful description of what it will look like when you get to where you want to be. Most importantly it can be used to evaluate whether you have achieved what you want to achieve.

I would respond to the manager above with encouragement but encourage him to flesh out what he wants to achieve:

Question: 'What would it look like if you had reached the sales that you want?'

Manager: 'Customers are happy to buy from any cashier and if any cashier leaves we can still maintain our sales figures easily.'

writing effective goals

- Write them as though we have already achieved the desired state. Not 'We will have...' but 'We have...'.
- Include success criteria by which we can measure our success.
- Include powerful emotive words about the benefits of achieving the desired state: 'in-depth', 'happy', 'excellent', 'good', 'easily'.

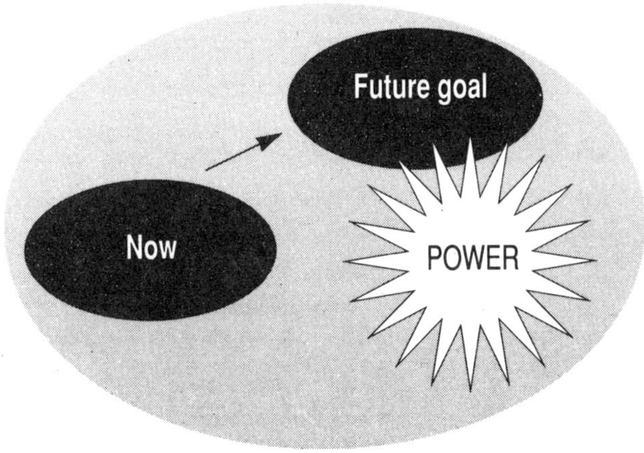

- Make it within your power to achieve, not dependent on others.
- What will you gain when you have achieved your goal?
- Does it allow for more than one way to achieve the outcome?
- Use words, pictures, feelings and reactions. Non-verbal information is the most powerful:

Powerful words	10%
Vivid pictures	20%
Strong emotion	30%
Action	40%

Remember these quotes:

> 'Words mean different things to different people.'
> 'Pictures are worth a thousand words.'
> 'It's not what you say, it's the way you say it.'
> 'Actions speak louder than words.'

One of the secrets of successful managers is that they leave people with inspiring goals and let them sort out how to get there themselves.

This is why goal setting is one of the key skills in coaching and empowerment. Take our team of cashiers, for example. The manager could leave it to them to sort out how to achieve the goal. He does not have to concern himself with the detailed action of how the Number 1 Cashier will coach the others, as long as everyone has bought into the goal and agreed to support each other to achieve it.

One final thing on goals. Gestalt psychology has shown us that when we arrive at our goal our energy is shut down except for the amount needed to maintain it. This is why we reach complacency after performance in the change cycle. So for managers it is essential to keep extending or changing our employees' goals.

The Peter Principle – that people reach their level of incompetence – is not true. What happens is that people reach the level of their goals – and then shut down.

One way to increase the power of action is to quantify what will happen if you do nothing about the problem. This provides the fear motivation, which combined with a strongly visualised goal will get virtually anyone to move. So the next step is to quantify the cost of the performance gap.

9

step 5 – what is the cost of the gap?

quantifying the gap

The gap is the difference between what is happening now and what we want to happen.

Ask:

'What would be the effect of doing nothing?'

or

'What will be the cost of the gap if it were to continue?'

Who	Doing Now	Want Them To Do
System (the branch)	20% below profit =£200k	hit profit target
	CSI .5	CSI .7
	second from bottom	top half of league
Cashier 1	doing all new sales	helping others sell

Customers	happy	happy to buy from any cashier
Other cashiers	no new sales	all making an equal contribution
Supervisor	not a proven seller	helps Anne to coach the others
Manager	worried that Anne might leave	happy that all cashiers can sell

The performance gap
£200,000 lost potential sales.
Vulnerable to Anne leaving
Manager loses bonus

You can see how important it is to have figures to compare in order to quantify the gap. If we had accepted 'poor' or 'terrible' it would have been much harder to quantify any gap. Similarly, if we had just concentrated on the Number 1 Cashier and not the whole system, it would have been hard to see the full effect of the gap.

If you cannot quantify the gap you might need to go back again to get more detail on what is happening now and what we want to happen. Some people find it useful to have a new piece of A3 paper for quantifying the gap. They use it landscape style and divide it up into two columns with a gap for the performance gap, eg:

What They Are Doing Now	Gap	What We Want Them To Do

Using different colours for the content of the different columns also works well.

Quantifying the gap can provide the ultimate fear motivation or disturbance to get people to move:

- *'Lawnmower sounds rough, how long has it sounded like that?'*
  'Oh, since I filled it up with petrol.'
  'Which can did you use?'
  'The green one.'
  'That could ruin your engine. A new one would cost £300.'
- *'I think we need more parking spaces.'*
  'Why?'
  'On Monday a customer could not find a space.'
  'Why?'
  'There was a bus strike and everyone came by car. Some people parked in the customer spaces.'
  'That was my best customer, she was on her way to give me a £30,000 order!'
- *'He is hopeless.'*
  'What do you mean by hopeless?'
  'His appearance is too scruffy for the front office. You actually see customers look at him and walk out.'
- *'I need some training.'*
  'Are you sure that you know what we expect from you?'
  'I assume it is to do X.'
  'No, it is to do 2 times X! And that is in your contract!'
- *'You need some training.'*
  'I know how to do it. It is just that I do not agree with our policy.'
  'It is an essential part of this job!'
- *'I need to improve my sales figures.'*
  'My conversion rate is high, I just need more appointments. I only have one month to reach my targets.'

- *'I need to lose weight so I am going to join Weight Watchers.'*
  'I eat too much junk food and snack between meals, and driving to work does not help. If I do not change my lifestyle I have a 50 per cent chance of having a heart attack.'
- *'Keep your head still when you swing.'*
  'You are looking up to see where the ball goes. You will never beat your brother.'
- *'This dehumidifier will reduce condensation.'*
  'When did the problem start?'
  'When we had double glazing fitted.'
  'The dehumidifier will cost £200 and the damp could cost much more. Open those windows!'

Notice the difference! You can feel the energy for action. Quantifying the gap will help overcome inertia and complacency. It also gives you valuable information about how much you can afford to spend on the solutions.

why is quantifying the gap so difficult?

The most common request for extra help that I get is on quantifying the performance gap. The problem is that we are entering the realms of change, of people's attachment to their current reality or fantasy, which has some emotional value or pay-off to them. No one likes it when it is pointed out that they are wrong. Do you? We do our best to protect our view of the world.

However, once we can identify the cost of a gap, we are more likely to do something about it. The next step is to find out the causes of that gap.

10

step 6 – what are the causes and potential solutions?

focusing on the key people

Quantifying the performance gap will give you a good idea of where the most crucial performance gaps are. You also need to focus on the key players involved. Ask yourself:

'If this is the cost of the gap, who are the most important people who affect this?'

Once we have identified the main culprits, we can start to investigate the causes for their behaviour. Do they lack knowledge, skills and motivation, or are there environmental factors stopping them from performing?

causes of low performance

Remember the main factors that affect a person's performance:

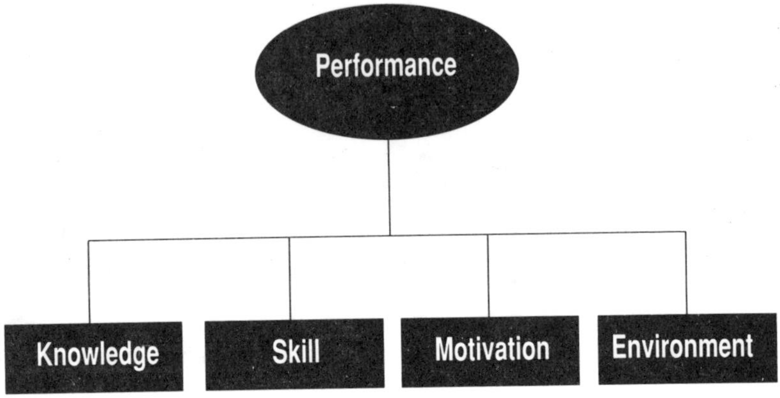

And the reasons for low performance:

- inadequate information or reference material;
- poor working environment or inadequate tools;
- poor incentives;
- lack of knowledge;
- lack of skill;
- poor motivation.

(Source: Thomas F Gilbert's Behaviour Engineering Model from *Human Competence*, 1978.)

Think about the key player or players who affect the performance gap. Have they got the:

- knowledge;
- skills;
- motivation;
- environment?

creativity techniques

If you remember, the instructions for step 6 were to generate as many solutions as possible and to 'suspend judgement as to their feasibility, and put them all down'. If you are not generating ideas freely, you might think of trying some other creative thinking techniques.

Think of the opposite of what you want:

> 'What would make this worse?'
> 'What would be the worst thing we could do?'

Try the wildest ideas:

> 'What would be the wildest idea we could do?'
> 'What if there were no limits?'

Think of analogies:

> 'If this person were a plant, what would I need to do to nurture him?'

Or similarities in different sectors:

> 'How do they overcome this situation in the airline industry?'

Think of high performers in this field from other sectors:

> 'The Church is good at conversions. How do they win their customers?'

Anything will do, give it a try. This stage is the creative stage. It should be marked by some tension relief, fun and laughter as you consider all the possible solutions without trying to evaluate any of them. Have fun...

checklist example

Let's take the cashier example forward to analyse the causes for the £200,000 performance gap and generate a list of potential solutions.

step 6 – what are the causes and potential solutions?

Try to generate as many solutions as possible, suspend judgement as to their feasibility, and put them all down in the right-hand column (or on your piece of paper). Think about the key player or players who affect the performance gap. Have they got the required knowledge and skills?

Question	Potential Solution
Do you think they lack some knowledge or skill?	No.
Can we make the performance easier in any way?	(Simplify the tasks? Split the job.)
Design checklists? Clarify performance standards?)	Provide a checklist about what to do when selling. Allow cashiers to specialise in certain areas.
Were they once able to do it?	No
Try practice, better information, and performance feedback.	Give them roleplay practice and feedback. Model the nine most popular sales situations. Encourage fellow cashiers to listen.

	Make sure the supervisor coaches and gives feedback.
Have they got the capability to learn how to do this?	Yes.
Consider training them or providing learning materials	Get the Number 1 Cashier to write a simple guide to selling. Organise some practical training around role plays.
If they haven't got the capability to learn to do this, can we transfer them to a job that they can do, or terminate their employment?	As the supervisor is not a proven seller, consider removing present supervisor. Train her in sales and coaching skills. Make the present number 1 cashier into the supervisor.

motivation

Do they get poor feedback on performance? Provide clear performance goals and regular feedback on positive as well as negative performance.	Break the sales target down into weekly goals. Put up a weekly achievement chart.
If they do it right, do they suffer in any way, eg by being given more work?	Reduce the punishment for high performance. Provide admin support for those who sell the most.
Introduce rewards and incentives.	Individual and team bonuses for achieving sales. Big night out for hitting team bonus.

Are they being rewarded for low performance?
Stop the rewards

No team bonus if you do not achieve your individual goals.

Do people lack self-esteem?
Help them visualise success, set positive goals

Break the team targets down to weekly goals.
Involve the cashiers in setting the lower and upper limits for their goals, eg between three and five sales per week each. Make it seem very achievable.

Catch people doing things right, build on success.

Support initial failure, reward effort.

environment

Is there anything wrong with their environment, methods, equipment?

Make sure that the cashiers share all the sale leaflets available.

Are the managers helping?

Make sure they can ask for cover to talk to customers for a little longer.

Improve management

The supervisor has no proven sales ability and does not have the knowledge and skills to coach staff in sales.

Any other obstacles?
Try to remove them

Define sales coaching as a key part of the job.
Appoint new supervisor with the competencies to do the job.

The questions generated too many solutions to handle! Do not worry about this now – we want as many as possible.

We will look at how to put all the possible solutions through a 'reality filter' in step 7.

11

step 7 – action plan

the reality filter

One of the reasons why you can afford to be creative and generate an enormous list of solutions in step 6 is because you know that there is another stage coming up when you will evaluate the feasibility of the solutions.

Remember step 7 of the checklist.

step 7 – action plan

Look at the list of possible solutions on the previous pages and agree them with your client. Cross out the options:

- that are just not feasible;
- of which the cost would be greater than the benefit.

Highlight the options:

- that can be easily implemented;
- that will give the best results for minimum effort.

So let's apply this to the list of solutions for the number 1 cashier. To save time we will only look at the first 10 of the potential solutions:

1. Provide a checklist about what to do when selling. *Yes*
2. Allow cashiers to specialise in certain areas? *No, they all need to cover*
3. Reassert that selling is an essential art of the cashier's job. *Yes, easy*
4. Give them some role play practice and feedback. *Possible*
5. Model the nine most popular sales situations. *Yes*
6. Encourage fellow cashiers to listen in and give supportive feedback. *Yes, easy*
7. Use feedback checklists on the front desk. *Yes*
8. Make sure the supervisor coaches and gives feedback. *But they lack skills*
9. Get the number 1 cashier to write a simple guide to selling. *Would have to make time*
10. Organise some practical training around role plays *Possible*

group solutions together

Ask:

'Can we group any of these things together?'
'What are the easiest things to do?'

The reality filter has probably started to combine solutions already.

Finally

Make sure that you add accountabilities and dates to the agreed actions; see below.

action plan

What	Who	When
1–1 session	manager and current supervisor	1st 10.00
Planning for team session	manager and current supervisor	5th 1.00–3.00
Team session	manager, supervisor and team	8th 9.00–12.00
Ask my boss for help with more achievable sales targets	my boss	this evening
Ring Marketing about better literature	me	this afternoon
Try these easier options, then review if supporting the existing supervisor is working	me and you	10th at 10.00

follow up

Set a date now to follow up on these actions 10/.../...

And a date when you can evaluate whether the gap has been closed 1/12/...

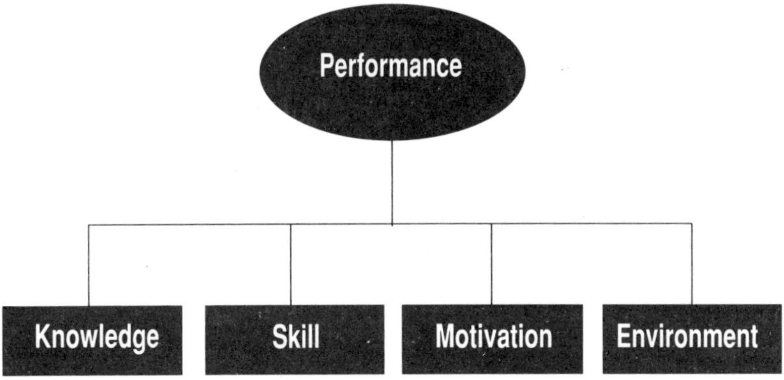

agreeing dates for review

You may have noticed that this action plan is very useful. It prompts you to set a date for review. Always agree the next action and gain commitment to a next step.

what happens if you do not write an action plan?

If you do not make a commitment to some action then you are wasting your time! You will probably prefer to avoid the discomfort of being pinned down to action, dates and a review but if you can get through this pain you will achieve what you want.

measuring success and keeping it going

Measuring success should be easy if you did a good job of pulling out measurable examples of what people are doing now and what you want them to do. A key part of many solutions is setting up the measurement of what you want to happen. This focus itself can be the only solution needed. What is measured tends to happen, eg:

Question: 'How can we measure customer service? It's subjective.'

Manager: 'Well, other companies do it. We can design a customer survey, do some mystery shopping – there are several ways of getting a customer service index. We could design a survey which we could use in August, then we could use it again after the solutions have been implemented and see if there has been any change.'

The action plan is the final part of the seven-step process.

12

summary and examples

recap

The key things to remember in each stage are:

1. What is the problem?
   - What is the presenting problem?
   - Clarify who the customer is: 'Who will this report go to?'
2. Who is involved?
   - Draw the system diagram.
   - Identify the key people to the performance gap.
3. What is happening now?
   - Start with the key people who affect the performance gap.
   - Find out how the key system (eg the branch) is performing.
   - Get down to something you can measure.
4. What do we want to happen?
   - Compare with what they are doing now.
   - Describe how you would like to see it.

   - Get specific measures.
   - Keep flipping between today and tomorrow.
   - Build up a picture of the two states.
5. What is the cost of the gap?

Quantify the
value of the gap

£

   - What is the effect of doing nothing?
   - How much will this cost?
6. What are the causes and potential solutions?
   - Suspend judgement.
   - Generate as many ideas as possible.
   - Be creative.
7. Action plan.

What	Who	When

   - Put all the ideas through the reality filter.
   - Which are too expensive?
   - Which are we best equipped to try?

- What will give us maximum effect for minimum effort?
- What shall we try first?
- Group solutions together.
- Agree what you need to do.
- When?
- Don't forget a time to review.

examples

example 1

Boss: 'Hey Mike, have you got five minutes? Can you get a quote for buying some new project management software? I saw some demonstrated at a conference, and I think it could help us.'

Manager: 'Sure, who is it for?'

Boss: 'My eight project managers.'

Manager: 'So what are they doing at the moment?'

Boss: 'Projects are running 10 per cent over budget.'

Manager: 'How much is that worth?'

Boss: 'Well, on a £10 million turnover that's £1 million.'

Manager: 'Is that the problem?'

Boss: 'Yes. We have no problem with quality or delivery dates, in fact the customer is delighted with us. It's just that we always go over budget and now that we have been taken over by the Americans they are sticklers for hitting budget.'

Manager: 'Could your project managers hit budgets before?'

Boss: 'Yes, they are all skilled project managers. I recruited them.'

Manager: 'So why don't they hit budget here?'

Boss: 'Well, I suppose we have always emphasised quality and delivery; a 10 per cent overspend has been accepted. The accountant and I always hold a 10 per cent contingency just in case.'

Manager: 'So why can't you continue to do that?'

Boss: 'The Americans won't accept any contingency, we have to hit budget.'

Manager: 'Have you told the project managers?'

Boss: 'No, but that won't solve the problem because most of the 10 per cent overspend is all overtime and the designers have come to expect it. If I just tell everyone to meet budget, the effect on morale could be catastrophic! We might lose out on quality and delivery.'

Manager: 'So the problem is how to maintain quality and delivery but get designers to do this with no overtime?'

Boss: 'Yes. The problem is that they have come to expect overtime payments as a large part of their pay packet.'

Manager: 'What could you do to resolve that?'

Boss: 'Got it! I could offer a project bonus for delivery on time to quality and budget that would more than offset the overtime they could earn. They would get the added benefits of more leisure time.

'Thanks, that really helps. I will brief the project managers tomorrow and they can introduce the changes. Thanks for your help.'

lessons

- The boss had a budget for new software.
- If he had bought the new software it would have been the wrong solution.
- You don't have to draw diagrams.
- The process does not have to take a long time.
- You can be flexible with the process.

example 2

Frank wants to lose weight.

- '*What is the problem?*'
  'I need to join Weight Watchers.'

'*No, that is a solution, what is the problem?*'
'I want to lose weight.'
'*Who is involved in this?*'
'My wife doesn't fancy me any more, I cannot keep up with my kids on the football pitch, and I have stopped rock climbing with a group of good friends because I am too unfit.'
'*What do you weigh now?*'
'I weigh 17 stone.'
'*What is your lifestyle like?*'
'I work hard, drive everywhere, have big business lunches, eat chocolate during the day and take no exercise.'
'*What would you like to be able to do?*'
'Be about 13 stone, look good, feel fit enough to play football with the lads and dads' team and go rejoin the climbing club.'
'*If you do nothing about this, what could happen?*'
'Divorce, heart attack, loneliness.'
'*Is it worth doing something about?*'
'You bet.'
'*Do you know how to live a healthy life?*'
'Yes, I used to be a PE teacher.'
'*Do you have the skill to keep fit?*'
'Yes, of course.'
'*What about motivation, feedback, rewards etc?*'
'Up to now Sue has been happy that I have earnt a lot of money, I have a very expensive company car which I drive the two miles to work, I do not really like football and I am getting a bit too old for rock climbing. All my colleagues are as-unfit as I am. We have a lunch club that we call the Teletubbies and I can put my business lunches on expenses. I suppose it's a motivation thing really.'
'*Could you walk to work, join a gym etc?*'
'Yes, I could walk to work, I could start playing golf

with my rock climbing mates. A few of them are joining a local club, and Sue would like to play too.'

'So what are you going to do?'

'I will aim for a healthy lifestyle rather than a diet. I will walk to work every day, trade my company car in for a pay rise and join the golf club with Sue. It has a gym too, and I am sure the boys would like the gym. I think I can get down to about 13 stone in about six months. No problem. Thanks for the chat.'

example 3

step 1 – what is the problem?

- Not the assumed solution – what is the real problem?
- 'How can the junior squash team win the league?'

step 2 – who is involved?

- Draw a diagram of all the people involved in the problem like the one shown on page 97.
- Put the key people in the centre.
- Make links between the key people.
- Label what is happening between them.

step 3 – what is happening now?

- Describe what is happening now.
- What are the key people doing now?
- Try to get facts, figures, anything measurable.

'We have a very good junior coaching scheme and some very good players. But when they get to 15 and 16, the boys tend to get involved with girls and other "cool" things. I am in danger of losing two of my best players again. We are second in the league and should be top.'

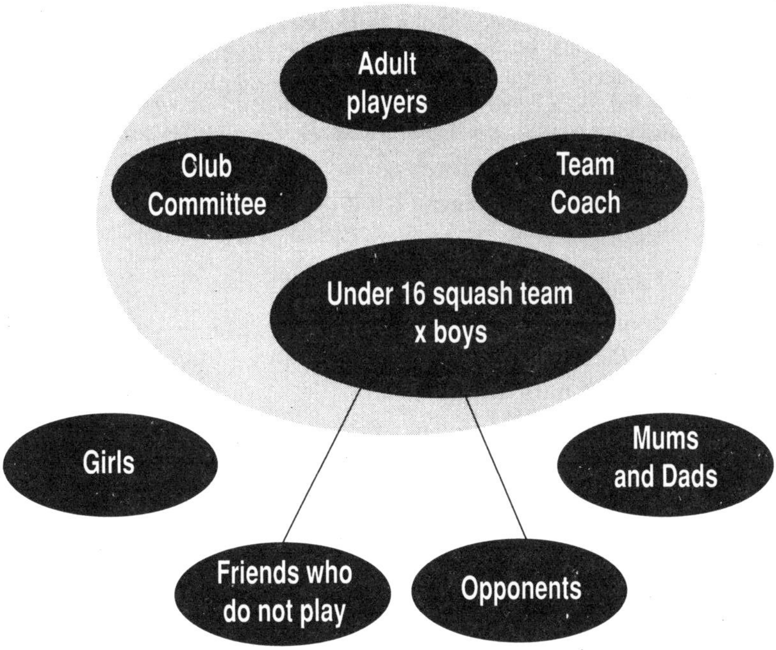

step 4 – what do we want to happen?

- Visualise how you would like things to be.
- How will you know when you have reached this state?
- Try to visualise a strong picture of what success looks like.

'I want to keep my two best players and win the league.'

step 5 – what is the cost of the gap?

- What would happen if you did nothing?
- Estimate the cost of the gap if it were to remain.
- If you cannot find a serious gap then consider leaving things alone!

> 'The junior coaching scheme has been going for five years. We have some very good players at all ages. But we have always just missed winning the league. This year is our best chance. The coaching scheme is held on a Saturday morning and the committee is under pressure to let the courts go to racket ball. I am worried that if we do not win something the juniors will drift away to other sports and interests.'

Let's have a look at the causes in a bit more detail.

step 6 – what are the causes and potential solutions?

Try to generate as many solutions as possible, suspend judgement as to their feasibility, and put them all down in the right-hand column. Think about the key player or players who affect the performance gap:

> 'Well, the key players in this appear to be the boys themselves and outside influences.'

Question	Potential Solution
Do you think they lack some knowledge or skill?	'They have the skill to win the league.'
Can we make the performance easier in any way?	Simplify the tasks? Split the job? Design checklists? Clarify performance standards?
Were they once able to do it?	'They used to be very keen on squash.' Try practice, better information, and performance feedback
Have they got the capability to learn how to do this?	'They do plenty of training. It is just getting them to stay that is the problem.'

	Consider training them or providing learning materials.
If they haven't got the capability to learn to do this, can we transfer them to a job that they can do or terminate their employment?	'We cannot attract new 16-year-old players. It is a national problem' 'If we cannot crack this problem the junior squash coaching might have to stop.'

motivation

Question	Potential Solution
Do they get poor feedback on performance?	Provide clear goals and regular feedback on positive as well as negative performance. 'I have told them that they are good enough to win the league. But after three close calls I think they have lost self-belief.'
If they do it right, do they suffer in any way, eg by being given more work?	'If they are serious they have to train hard and miss out on going to the cinema, discos etc.' Reduce the punishment for high performance. Introduce rewards and incentives.
Introduce rewards and incentives	'Yes, if we had a disco at the squash club, or a place to meet girls after training, that would please them. Perhaps we could change some training to early Friday evening and organise local discos for just after training.'

Are they being rewarded for low performance?	Stop the rewards. 'Hmm ... If we made it so that they could only come to the disco if they do the training ...'
Do they lack self-esteem?	'Yes, we need to inspire them again. I will ask our local international player to come and give them a session. I will tell him to tell them how good he thinks they are.' Help them visualise success, set positive goals. Catch people doing things right, build on success.

environment

Is there anything wrong with their environment, methods, equipment?	'I will ask them when they want to train and negotiate with the committee for us to use the glass backed courts.'
Are the managers helping?	'Girls are the key. I will set up a squash social and disco club and get the parents and the girls involved.' Improve management. 'I can see that a lot it is down to me.' Any other obstacles? Try to remove them.

step 7 – action plan

Look at the list of possible solutions in the right-hand column.

Cross out those:

- that are just not feasible;
- of which the cost would be greater than the benefit.

Highlight those:

- that can be easily implemented;
- that will give the best results for minimum effort.

Of those that are left, can you combine them into things that go together?

Now agree which order to do things. Make an action plan of the solutions you are going to try:

What	Who	When
Propose social and disco club	me	Friday
Talk to the committee about using the glass back courts	me	Thursday
Talk to the boys about the problem	me	Friday

Set a date for review:

'I will keep this plan and review it on finals day when we win the league.'

some tips

The process will not help you to improve your employees' performance on its own. Remember that non-verbal messages have more impact than words. The way you approach people will be as important as the process that you use to analyse their problems.

You will need to apply all your basic skills of:

- questioning;
- listening;
- empathy;
- analysis;
- synthesis;
- creativity; and
- working systematically.

However, perhaps what will be most important is the way you tackle the task of analysing your employees' performance. We have some enabling beliefs that help us to be an excellent performance consulting firm (with thanks to Julia and Peter Block).

Our role is to:

- use a rational and fair process;
- know where we are in that process;
- reflect back reality to the client;
- be authentic at all times;
- help the client face problems.

We believe that:

- everyone wants to do a good job;
- there are reasons why people do not perform;
- we can analyse these reasons and design solutions that work;
- part of our purpose is to help people see the real causes of problems so that they can overcome them for ever;
- no one performs in isolation;
- single solutions do not work;
- many problems are caused by inappropriate solutions to old problems;
- if you face up to problems they often disappear;
- the best way is being lean, efficient, cost-effective, doing only what is needed.

I hope that, by sharing some of these values with you, you may take some of them on board and they will help you to be effective in your role as a manager.

summary

Well there it is. A process for analysing any performance problem and raising anyone's performance. And, if you use it sensitively and skilfully you will be a very effective manager.

Just having a process is very powerful and you should get major successes with your people if you follow a common process. After that, the value you add depends on your skill and confidence. It is often said that a consultant acts like a mirror (someone who borrows your watch to tell you the time). This story is partly true because part of our role is to reflect reality back to the client and not take the problem away from them. In behaving like this, one has to be pretty tough; your people actually want you to take the problem away, and resisting this can elicit projected anger, however polite.

Behaving as a diagnostic problem solver is not easy. Some key tips:

- Emphasise the joint problem solving approach.
- Share the process with your people.
- Trust your feelings.
- If things seem to be going wrong, say so.
- Use your feelings as information, give a feelings commentary.
- Your first performance problem to solve is your competence and credibility in working with this process with your people.

We have started a network of people who use our approach. If you have any queries, would like to chat through issues or find details of our skill workshops and masterclasses, find us on our Web site at www.actconsult.co.uk.

Good luck!

Nigel Harrison

a story

This is an account of putting the process into action to improve the performance of a sports centre. (All characters and events are pure fiction.)

the mission

Councillor Harris had had it in for me since my appointment as the youngest manager in the city. He had said that I was too inexperienced and he wanted a long-standing council employee called Stan Overthrow to get the job. Since then I had taken over Bramble Lane Leisure Centre in Sheffield and had made it the most successful local authority leisure centre in the city.

Harris had recently been appointed Head of Leisure Services and I felt wary when I received a phone call from his secretary asking me to attend a meeting of the Leisure Sub-committee. When I heard the words, 'You have done such a good job at Bramble Lane, we know you will be able to do it', I was reminded of the psychological game that Eric Berne calls NIGYSOB: *Now I've Got You, You Son Of a Bitch*. My immediate thoughts were, 'Beware of people setting you up, what do they really want?'

Harris beamed. 'Congratulations. We want you to transfer to Tootley and implement the things you have done at Bramble Lane; we need to turn it around in six months. It should be easy for a man with your ability. Stan can take over from you at Bramble Lane as he is overdue for a promotion.'

So that was it: if Stan took my job he would inherit the most successful leisure centre in the city. In our annual performance review he would look great whilst I would have a struggling unit. Harris would be able to say that I had been lucky at Bramble Lane, and that my methods had failed at Tootley. I had to think quickly. I knew that Tootley was a 10-year-old sports and leisure centre with a pool, gym and sports hall. Deliberately avoiding Harris, I asked the whole committee: 'What is the problem you want me to solve?'

Danny, a sensible councillor, said: 'It is just as Harris has described it. We need to turn around the performance of Tootley or at least show that it can make a profit to avoid having to sell it off.' I asked: **'Who is involved in this project?'**

'Well, the 15 staff who might lose their jobs. The city accountant is looking at the option of selling the centre to "SportFitness" who have made a bid of £2 million for the site. Oh yes, the present manager, Eric Fitzpatrick, has retired on grounds of stress.' I asked: 'Who would the new manager report to?' Harris replied: 'You would report to this committee on a monthly basis.'

I asked: **'So what is the performance of Tootley at the moment?'** The city accountant replied: 'The forecast loss for the year is £140,000, they have had no manager for six weeks, and no effective management for two years. The building is in a good state. The solution seems to be to appoint a good manager, which is why we have come to you.'

I asked: **'So what do you want to see happening at Tootley?'** 'Strong management, some discipline', Harris almost shouted across the room. I turned to face the accountant. 'What would success look like to you?' He replied: 'Well, a loss of £50,000 this year would be acceptable if we can show improvement to at least break even by next year. The important thing is that I must show it as an asset over two years to avoid this pressure to sell.'

I turned to Danny. **'What would success look like to you, Councillor?'** He was passionate in his reply: 'We save the employees' jobs and continue to provide an affordable sports centre for the people of Tootley.' This had struck a nerve with Danny. The feeling in his reply meant something.

I decided to probe further, asking: **'What is the worst that could happen if things were to remain as they are?'** Danny replied instantly: 'We do not want another expensive, exclusive health club which most of my constituents cannot afford.' 'What could that mean to you?' I asked. 'With local elections coming up at the end of the year I might lose my seat', came the honest reply.

'And what about you?' I asked the accountant. 'Short-term sale of an asset is a poor solution. I want to build up profitable council assets, not sell them off. If you can help us achieve this I will be very grateful.'

Finally I turned to Harris; his answer was: 'Well, we won't leave things as they are. If you won't take the job the most senior person who is due for promotion is Stan, so he would have to try to sort it out.'

I tried to summarise the performance gap as I saw it: 'So this is about saving 15 people's jobs, Danny's seat on the council, £140,000 in cost and avoiding losing a city asset to private hands?' 'Yes', came the subdued reply. 'And we only have six months.' 'Is it okay if I ask some questions about the causes of this low performance?' I asked. 'Go ahead,' said Danny. 'Harris knows the details; he appointed the last manager, two years ago.'

I turned to Harris. 'Tootley is only 10 years old and seems in pretty good shape to me.' 'Yes, we spent £200,000 last year on a major refit because we thought that would get the people back in, but it made no difference.' 'Did it ever make a profit?' I asked. 'Yes, for the first eight years.' 'What happened after eight years?' I asked. 'Well, we appointed Eric, a good chap, but costs seem to have soared and attendance is down.' 'So you think the main cause is Eric's poor management?' I probed. 'Yes, I suppose so, he turned out not to be strong enough to control the staff.' 'So you want me to control the staff', I questioned. Harris blustered: 'Yes, I mean no... just do what you did at Bramble Lane!'

I quickly reviewed my position. I needed room to manoeuvre and I did not want to get trapped in a solution that might be a total assumption. Perhaps the problem was outside the control of the manager? I did not want to lose my job at Bramble Lane and hand over a successful venture and all the praise to Stan. The performance league table for sports centres was out at the end of the year and I wanted to be top. I knew quite a lot about how important this was to the committee, so I would make them a proposal.

I looked at the accountant and Danny: 'Here is my proposal. We do not know the reasons why Tootley is losing money, so new management may not be the answer. I have an excellent deputy at Bramble Lane in Sara, who could do with the experience of running the centre with a little coaching. I propose that she takes over my role at Bramble Lane on probation. I will take over as acting manager at Tootley and come back to you with my proposals for improving its performance within one week. If you agree to support these proposals I will take on the job and implement the proposals by the end of the year. I will be manager of both centres with a pay rise for Sara and myself. If we break even by the end of the year I want to be made area manager.' 'Out of the question!' said Harris. 'Will you give us a few minutes to consider your proposal?' said Danny. I left the room as Danny and the accountant prepared to face Harris.

I thought I had done well and this was confirmed in five minutes when Danny called me back. 'We agree to your proposal,' he said, and with a wink he added, 'I think the people of Tootley will be very grateful to you when you save their sports centre.'

'And your seat', I thought.

Well, that was it. I left the meeting, told Sara the news (she was delighted), and prepared to visit Tootley Sports and Leisure Centre that evening as a customer before anyone knew who I was.

my first visit to the sports centre

That night I took my two children to the sports centre. But first, I left work early and on my way home I dropped in to the new 'SportFitness' centre that had opened near the local big Tesco. I asked about membership and facilities and was given a glossy brochure by a very attractive young woman receptionist. Membership was £42 per month and included towels, all classes and access to a gym and 20-metre pool. The joining fee was £100 but there was a special offer this week of two for the price of one. Family membership was £90 per month. Everything looked spick and span and very modern. The centre was located very near to Tootley commuter village and on most people's way home from work after a visit to Tesco. This was the opposition.

I managed to get home early and told Julie, my wife, about the new job. She was very suspicious. 'But you have such a good team at Bramble, it has taken you so much effort to build it up, I do not want you working ridiculous hours.' I promised not to spend any more time on Tootley than I worked already. She was sceptical. I said I would take the children to the Tootley sports centre before tea. I wanted to experience the centre as a customer.

Arriving at Tootley Leisure Centre I was impressed. The building was new, the car park clean, large and empty. We parked near the door and approached the reception desk. A man and a woman were waiting to be served. Two elderly receptionists were talking to each other. I listened in: 'I don't know where the badminton rackets are, Madge, you had better page John.' A tannoy announcement soon boomed out: 'John to reception please, John to reception please.' One of the ladies turned to the couple. 'Won't be long now, we just need to see if we have any rackets; you wanted to book one court?' The other receptionist ignored all of us and seemed to be busy with some paperwork. The first receptionist, whom I had noticed was called Madge, now turned around to gossip with her colleague: 'Ooh, that John, where is he? He is always missing when you need him.' She was obviously waiting for John before she served any of us.

I interrupted: 'Excuse me, would you mind letting us in to the pool whilst you are waiting for John?' The couple nodded but Madge said: 'Sorry sir, I am serving this customer, you will just have to wait.' Normally I would have argued but this time I deferred and waited to see just how long it would be before we were seen.

It took 20 minutes to get access to the pool, which cost £8.00 for two children and myself. We were told that the session had started 20 minutes earlier and that we would have to be out in 40 minutes when the next session started. I asked for details of classes, joining the gym, pool times etc. I was told that there were no classes, you needed an assessment to join the gym and all details of process etc were out of print. I was recommended to ring for pool times; the number was in the *Yellow Pages*.

When we got in the pool it was lovely, the water was warm, the place was clean, the lifeguard looked very smart and friendly, and we virtually had the place to ourselves. After we finished swimming we changed in smart, clean, warm changing rooms. This place is not bad, I thought. On the way out of the changing rooms the kids asked for their customary chocolate: 'Can we have a drink of hot chocolate please, Dad?' She asked in that peculiar way kids have when they really want something. I asked if there was a café or a drinks machine.

'No love, we had a machine but people caused such a mess with their litter – some people are ignorant – we had it taken out; the place is much tidier now, and anyway it will be your teatime soon, kids, you don't want to spoil your appetite.' As we left reception I glanced at the other receptionist; the paperwork that she was so busy with was *Hello* magazine.

'I think I will start looking at the performance of reception', I said to myself as I walked out.

starting to analyse the problem with the team

The next day I arrived at 8.30 am to start my performance review of Tootley Leisure Centre as the acting manager. I called the senior receptionist, instructor, cleaner and maintenance staff together in my office. After the introductions I asked who worked at the centre. I drew a large picture of the reception area, sports hall, gym and swimming pool, maintenance workshop, storeroom and boiler room.

On the picture I asked them to put all the people who worked in the different sectors. Then I asked them to label their hours of work. I then put the customers on the diagram, walking to the centre. My PA, Sheila, had figures for the number of customers; most were families (65 per cent).

I asked for the picture of customers two years ago compared with today. We drew two pictures up on the flip chart. The difference was startling.

Two years ago there had been 2,000 visitors a month, now there were 1,000 a month. The peak times last year had been lunchtimes, just after work, Saturdays and Sunday mornings. Now the peak time was Saturday. We were closed on Sunday. We used to take £12,000 per month two years ago; now, despite price rises, we were taking £8,000 per month. Staff numbers two years ago had been 8 full-time and 6 part-time, now there were 10 full-time only. All of this was news to my new colleagues; they had no idea how the centre was doing.

They were pleased with the recent refit, which they saw as a sign of confidence in the centre. They were especially proud of the cleanliness and smartness of the building. I explained that we needed at least to break even by the end of the year to survive. I said that I needed their help and was trying to find out the reasons for the financial gap before we implemented any solutions. I promised to involve them in the solutions and asked for their help in the investigation. I said that the first things I wanted to investigate were why visitor numbers were down and why labour numbers were up.

I arranged a meeting that afternoon between the two receptionists and my PA, who also looked after marketing. It was to be an interesting meeting.

sorting out reception

That afternoon I met Madge and Joyce in a new situation. They both failed to recognise me from the evening before; perhaps it was the suit and lack of children. I had some preconceived ideas about their perception of the quality of their customer service but I was determined not to let these prejudice my analysis; it may be that they just did not know what was expected of them. We held the meeting in reception at a quiet period, but I insisted that one of the instructors covered the desk for any customers who came in. My PA, Sheila, had lots of information about customer visits etc.

Again I used a flip chart and asked them to draw a picture of reception. They put Madge and Joyce in the centre of the diagram and stopped. 'That's it', said Madge. 'We are Reception, except after 5.00 of course when the instructors stand in, but they like the overtime, you know; we are 9–5, and we do not work weekends.' I asked them to put their hours on the diagram and the hours of the instructors.

Then I asked Sheila to put the customers on the diagram and

the hours of peak activity. These were after 5.00 and Saturday mornings. It was obvious that reception was manned by part-time staff at the busiest hours. I had visited at 4.30 the evening before, which was why Madge had greeted me. I asked them how they saw things at the moment. 'Well, from what you said this morning, we only have 600 visitors a month and that is not enough, but we can't do anything about that', said Madge. 'Yes, it would be nice to get back to the numbers we had two years ago, it was a much more noisy place, you know; everything is much smarter now but I miss the buzz, we always had two reception kiosks working, now we only use one.'

I asked if they would mind answering some questions about customers. We would put the answers on one flip chart called Now and have another for Future. I fired off the questions based on my experience of good reception and marketing at Bramble and my knowledge of private leisure clubs.

The conversation went like this:

'Do we have a membership scheme?' 'No.'
'Do we have a brochure?' 'No.'
'Do we run classes?' 'No.'
'Do we provide free towels?' 'No, of course not, that would be expensive!'
'Do we have a café?' 'No.'
'Do we have a drinks or snack machine?' 'No.'
'Do we offer personal trainer sessions?' 'No.'
'Do we have a code of customer practice?' 'No.'
'Have you been trained in customer service?' 'No.'
'Have you been trained in how to give customer service?' 'No.'
'Are experienced receptionists on duty over the peak times?' 'No.'
'Do we do special offers?' 'No.'
'Do we do lane swimming at lunchtime for workers?' 'No, we used to.'

'Do we market ourselves?' 'Yes, but only in the *Yellow Pages*.'
'What do customers say about our prices?' 'They say we are expensive.'

To cut a long story short, Madge, Joyce, Sheila and I agreed an action plan to try to attract more customers and treat them well when they arrived. Madge and Joyce said they had never been consulted like this before. They both agreed to visit the local private leisure centre that evening to get ideas. They seemed enthused by the challenge.

Before they got too carried away, I set my expectations of how they should treat customers from that point on. 'Our job is to exceed the customer's expectations, to make sure they have an enjoyable visit, will come again and will tell their friends to come too. I want you to share our ideas for improvement with customers and ask them what they think. We are to start the new discounts and schemes immediately. I want you to write up a rough sheet of new charges and offers. I also want you to stay late tonight to cope with the 5.00 peak and then come in late tomorrow.' I was surprised and warmed by their reaction. They seemed like new people. That night the reception area was a changed place.

What we had agreed was:

- A special offer of unlimited use of the leisure centre for £24 per month or £44 for a family ticket. We made a big banner and stuck it on the outside of the leisure centre. I also went on the radio to publicise the new scheme.
- A special lunchtime fitness session for workers, lane swimming, circuit training and fitness assessment. We made a small flyer and Sheila and Madge distributed them to the local offices.
- Joyce and Madge agreed to alter their hours permanently to 11.00 till 6.00 and they came in on Saturday

mornings. This was on the same salary; we did not inform the council, we just did it. We installed a drinks and snack machine in the reception area and Madge arranged for a local company to supply freshly made cakes and flapjacks to be sold at reception.

- Two reception desks were to be open at all times and if customers were queuing more than two deep Madge and Joyce were to call me or Sheila or the instructors to staff the third reception desk. In return, Madge would help Sheila with her work when things were slack.

I agreed to draft out a brochure that evening on my computer. We would print this at the office on coloured paper and use it until Sheila could get a proper one printed.

I left the centre that evening at 6.00 just as Madge and Joyce were finishing. They looked happy and I was confident that our proposals would bring in more people. Tomorrow I would look at why our labour costs were so high. That might be more difficult to sort out.

the instructors

The next morning I awoke early and had plenty of time to think about the day ahead. I had arranged to meet Sheila and our auditor at 9.00 in my office, then at 10.30 I would meet half of the instructors and at 2.30 the other half. I already knew that the instructors' salary bill was the biggest outgoing for the centre. This could be tough. As council workers they probably had very secure employment rights and I knew that they had a strong union. There are also statutory requirements for staffing, eg ratio of trained lifeguards to customers and the need to have first-aiders available. I was going to have to consider all these things.

At 9.00, I returned to my picture of the centre stuck on the wall. The auditor's name was Alan. 'Let me check a few things that I found out yesterday, Alan.' I started to point to the diagram of the instructors at the centre. 'Staff numbers two years ago were 8 full-time and 6 part-time and how much did they cost?' '£140,000,' Alan replied, 'now there are 10 full-time only and they cost £240,000.'

I was astounded. 'So this increase in costs was at the same time as we were getting fewer customers through the door and it accounts for half the shortfall?'

Alan shuffled through sheets of finely typed figures. 'Yes, it seems that two years ago we used casual student labour in school holidays to meet the peaks in school holiday attendance. We only need eight full-time staff as a core to run the centre during normal demand. That is to say, 2,000 visitors a month, not the 1,000 we have now. There are a minimum number of instructors to meet the regulations and workload for 1,000 visitors a month, so we could get away with a minimum of six.' 'And we have 10?' I replied. 'Yes.' Alan was very matter of fact about this. 'Why do we have 10? What happened over the past two years?' I asked. Alan replied: 'Ah, well, you see, the last manager took the opportunity to offer full-time jobs to some students who were very good. The staff also used to work strange working hours, starting at mid-day and finishing at 7.00 pm, plus every second Saturday, and we used to open on Sunday morning. The unions did not like the difficult hours and negotiated a 9–5 standard council working week. As a result we needed more staff to cover for peak times and more wages to pay overtime for after-hours working and weekend work. Also, income went down when we closed on Sunday mornings; they used to be very popular.'

I put my head in my hands. This was going to be harder than I thought. 'Do the instructors know we cannot afford to pay this wage bill?' I asked. 'No, I do not think they know how serious this is.' Alan then offered me some help. 'Two of them are eligible for early retirement but only one has expressed any interest. If they knew the centre might be sold they would probably leave and we could go back to eight full-time staff and start up the part-time mix again.' 'Alan, you are a genius,' I said, 'will you join me in two meetings with the instructors?' He agreed. The rest of the week was spent in negotiation with the instructors.

Once they realised that the centre would close if we could not reduce the wage bill, the two old hands volunteered for early retirement. I actually hired them back again to cover for peak periods. We also created a mentor role for the newly retired instructors to offer coaching to students whom we employed during school holidays. With their pension, cash payoff and part-time work, the retirees were delighted. My problem might be with the survivors. I had eight instructors with only enough work for six. I was confident that my marketing and changes to reception would bring in more customers and I told the team that I wanted to keep all of them if they would agree to some flexible working.

I explained what we were trying to do and said that I wanted to go back to their old contracts. They would lose overtime but they could be more flexible about their hours, which would be reduced by three hours a week. I was also starting to offer personal trainers to our customers. Instructors could take 20 per cent of any extra fees generated from this new income. Eventually the instructors came round and all agreed to the new way of working. In fact, two of them wanted to work part-time anyway. One was an Olympic hopeful swimmer and wanted to do more training, so we gave him free access to the pool; the other had a painting and decorating business. So all in all everything worked out very well. I worked out that we would reduce our wage bill to break even if we got our visitor numbers back up to 2,000. This should be possible: at Bramble Lane we had 2,500 per month.

That night I felt tired but satisfied. I had identified some of the main causes of low performance of the centre as a whole but was it enough to transform its performance? It was too early to say. I would need to be there to reinforce the message and keep the pace of change going. Like a football manager taking over a new club, my first impact had been quite dramatic. Everyone had responded much better than I had imagined. The rude old ladies on reception turned out to be friendly, creative assets. The tough unionised instructors turned out to like the flexible way of working. 'One should never make assumptions about people', I thought.

The reasons that they had not been performing had not been deliberate. It was about lack of knowledge, of expectations and information about the reality of their situation. I had helped them to face this reality, to focus on two main causes for the problem and face up to the necessary action to overcome the main problems. There were other problems that still existed, particularly the low performance of two of the instructors, but I felt it would work because I had helped the staff to face up to their problems and share in the solutions rather than imposing my own.

This made me think the problems at Bramble Lane had been to do with a poor building and the lack of skill of the staff. It was a good thing that I had not done what Harris suggested and implemented a renovation and training programme. They would have been totally the wrong solutions for Tootley.

improving the performance of two instructors

When I had taken the Tootley job I had asked for the performance reviews of all the staff. Two of the instructors, Bill and Ted, had very poor ratings in their performance reviews (PR) even though their boss, Eric, seems to have been a very easy-going manager. The other signature on the PR was John Noble, Chief Instructor. I had arranged to see John the next morning.

I had set aside two hours to spend with John on this

performance problem. We sat side by side at the conference room table and I had several large pieces of A3 paper so that we could draw diagrams of the problem. We started by drawing a picture of the centre. Bill and Ted both worked in the gym, which was the other side of reception from the sports hall and the swimming pool.

'Who do they report to?' I asked. 'Me', John replied. 'Where do you fit on the diagram?' It was very interesting that John pointed to the sports hall and when I asked him to draw himself on the diagram he put himself above the sports hall and the swimming pool. 'Why have you put yourself over these areas?' I asked. 'Because they have more staff and more customers and need more attention', he replied. I was already getting the impression that Bill and Ted were perhaps receiving less attention than their colleagues.

'Tell me about what is happening now with Bill and Ted', I asked. John frowned. 'Well, they are not very conscientious. Bill does not seem to care less and Ted is too friendly with customers and never does his paperwork. I have a tough time getting them to meet my standards, they are just not satisfactory.' 'Have we any evidence of this performance?' I asked. 'Yes, there have been three complaints about Bill's rudeness from customers and Ted's assessment sheets are a month behind.' 'How have you dealt with this so far?' I asked. 'Well, the gym is on the other side of the building from the pool and hall so I do not get much time to see them. We had their performance review a couple of months ago and I forced Eric to rate them down. I have also told them that they are not good instructors and I try to catch them doing things wrong and tell them off, what else can I do?'

It seemed to me that John's supervision style might have something to do with the problem. I had better help him see a positive side to the problem. 'What would it look like if things were working well?' I asked. John had a very clear idea. 'Well, I could walk into the gym at any time and get a smiling reception, Bill would be attentive to customers and Ted would have a nice neat pile of up-to-date assessments without me having to shout at him to get them done. Oh yes, and we would have no complaints from customers.'

'If we do nothing about this what will happen?' I asked. Again John was very quick to answer. He had obviously been going through this problem in his mind, and it was obviously worrying him.

I took a new sheet of paper and wrote two headings *1. Possible causes of the problem, 2. Possible solutions.* I agreed with John that we would spend some time investigating all the possible reasons for the present state of affairs. I will not trouble you with the whole conversation, but I did ask John if he had had any training in supervision and motivation, and the answer was no. He also admitted that he was a qualified PE instructor and swimming coach but was not qualified on all the new gym equipment. I thought this might be significant, as John had no problems with the pool and sports staff. I probed about the differences in the way he treated them compared with Bill and Ted. You could see throughout our conversation that he was recognising that he actually treated Bill and Ted differently from the others. This was partly due to location and partly his lack of knowledge about what they did.

As the message was soaking in about his involvement in the problem, I asked John about possible causes for Ted's behaviour. It turned out that he might not know about the council's customer service charter; we thought he had the skills to be pleasant because he was very popular with people who worked in the centre. As far as motivation went, this was probably the most important reason for his behaviour, as he didn't get any immediate feedback on his behaviour with customers. We decided to instigate customer feedback sheets after each fitness assessment. Finally, he had often complained to John that the gym needed rearranging and was badly laid out.

I made a note of all these possible causes and John agreed to talk to Bill to find out more. I took another sheet of paper and started on Ted. By now John was getting the hang of it. He wrote down the column headings and asked me: 'What are the main categories that affect performance?' 'Knowledge, skills, motivation and environment', I replied.

He wrote these down and started to tell me about Ted. 'His problem is paperwork. He may not know how to do it; he probably puts it off until the end of the day – it is better to schedule five minutes at the end of each session and do it as you go along; we could actually design the form better; his writing skill may be poor; if we changed it to multiple choice that might help him. I think he is motivated because he wants to do a good job, but the environment may not be right, he could do with a clipboard so he can make notes as he goes around the gym, and a filing cabinet might help.'

John had unwittingly come up with most of the solutions to Bill and Ted's problems himself. I gave him a bit of advice about coaching people. He agreed to talk to each of them separately and agree an action plan. He was going to support them and arranged to visit at a set time each morning and afternoon. He was also going to ask them to train him on the new equipment. I also gave him a book on empowerment and asked him to try to catch them doing something right and report to me so that I could give them some positive feedback. John and I agreed to formally review his progress with Bill and Ted in one month's time and informally every day.

Two weeks later he came into my office. 'Bill and Ted would like to show you the improvements they have made in the gym', he said. As I walked around that afternoon, listening with satisfaction as Bill showed me how he had reorganised the layout of the gym and how they had a new customer feedback card, Ted showed me the new multiple choice fitness assessment form and filing cabinet and how their gym was just as good as 'SportFitness' and how they had started to do personal trainer sessions. 'And we are even training John', they said with a smile.

'Well done, John', I said. I realised that he had managed to get across what he wanted to and that Bill and Ted thought it was their idea; surely that is the mark of a good supervisor. You will not be surprised to hear that John, Bill and Ted all got excellent ratings in their PR this year.

success

It is now the end of the year and Tootley has met its targets. We have made a small profit of £7,000 and are safe from takeover. The accountants have let me spend some of the money on a celebration party for the staff, the local residents and members of our Gold Card Scheme. Now I am the area director I have six leisure centres to look after. Fortunately, three are running very well: Bramble Lane, Tootley and Upperthorpe. Danny returns from the bar with a drink for me. 'I suppose you will be visiting your new centres that are not performing next.'

'No,' I answer, 'I want to visit Upperthorpe first to see what they are doing right!' I might learn something from them to help the others.'Then you know me, Danny. I will make no assumptions, just take each problem in turn and see if I can find the causes; after that, solutions are easy. Cheers!'

Well, perhaps it's not that simple, I thought. What had I done? Throughout my time at Tootley I had been very aware of the need to work quickly and focus on the real causes of the problem. (Harris had shown how expensive making assumptions could be by wasting £200,000 on refitting a nearly new building.) I had also tried to think about the people involved in the problem, where they are now and where they want to be. 'What will be the effect of doing nothing?' seems to be a good question to get people to think. I also looked for the causes of the gap, which gave me the solutions. The next bit was sticking to the action plan and seeing it through. Perhaps the most important thing I had done was not to assume that the performance problems were due to inadequate people; it always seems that way but almost never is.

As I made a mental note of these steps, I realised that I could repeat them for any problem. I will try them for my four new sports centres. Perhaps I can even improve the performance of Upperthorpe. Funny, I seem to have found a universal process for improving employee performance – perhaps I will write a book about it one day!

Bibliography

Block, P (1981) *Flawless Consulting*, Pfeiffer and Co, San Francisco

Carnegie, D (1964) *How to Win Friends and Influence People*, Simon & Schuster, New York

Carter et al (1984) *Systems, Management and Change*, Open University, Buckingham

Gilbert, Thomas F (1978) *Human Competence: Engineering worthy performance*, McGraw Hill

Knight, S (1995) *NLP at Work*, Nicholas Brealey Publishing, London

Mager, RF and Pipe, P (1984) *Analysing Performance Problems*, Lake Publishing Company

Rackham, N and Carlisle, J (1978) The behaviour of successful negotiators, *JEIT*, 2 (6)

Robinson, DG and Robinson, JC (1995) *Performance Consulting*, Berret-Koehler Publishers Inc, San Francisco